THE HAUNTED SOUTHLAND

GHOSTS OF SOUTHERN CALIFORNIA

BY
RICHARD SENATE

ILLUSTRATED
BY
SANDRA LARA

FORWARD
BY
ARTHUR MYERS

THE HAUNTED SOUTHALAND

by
Richard L. Senate

Illustrated By: Sandra Lara

Edited by: Jane Gilbert

Published by
Charon Press
(805) 643-3969

Charon Press
Ventura, CA.

Printed In U.S.A.

Second Edition 1994

Library of Congress Catalog Number: TX 3 641 843

ISBN 0-9640065-0-2 softcover

The author wishes to thank the following individuals in their help
in putting together this work,-

Patty Spielman
Peggy Richards
Brian Black
Brian Cloniger
Arroyo Grande Ghost Hunters
John Whyman
Delores Deilh
Marge O'Brien

Special Thanks to
Jane Gilbert for editing my manuscript
and my wife, Debbie Christenson Senate whose psychic gifts
have opened many doors to the other world.

Dedicated to the memory of
Leonard E. Senate
and
Sylvia Reynolds Senate
who gave me my love of the unknown.

The Illustrator wishes to thank Tommy Lee Edwards for the
career inspiration.

Contents

Forward

A TRIBUTE TO A REAL GHOST HUNTER

Richard's path and mine first crossed while I was writing a book about celebrities who have seen ghosts or who are ghosts themselves. One of these, the old movie actor Clifton Webb, seemed to be inhabiting the home of a California psychic named Kenny Kingston. Richard was shooting a TV show at Kingston's home, and came across a magnificent chair that had belonged to Webb. Debbie Senate, Richard's psychic wife, decided to sit in the chair. For her trouble, she got a slap in the face, a torn bodice and a bit of a scare. Kingston, who had been out of the room, returned hastily and said, "Clifton doesn't like women sitting in his chair."

Since then, when I need a good West Coast haunting for a book, I call Richard and he never fails to clue me in. I particularly like the one that he has recorded in this book. It's the last chapter, titled "My first ghost." He tells of encountering a ghostly monk in an old Spanish Mission.

"That's what got me involved in all this nonsense," he told me. "Before that, I was relatively sane."

Richard is a man who goes out looking for ghosts. He's a true parapsychologist. When I hear of the things he does it me feel like an imposter. I'm just an over the hill investigative reporter. I wait for other people to have ghostly experiences and then cross examine them. Only occasionally am I on hand when ghosts are walking, and even then I rarely notice it.

But Richard actually prowls through the bowels of the Queen Mary, now ignominiously docked at Long

Beach. He wanders through the mansion of the early movie hero, William S. Hart. He holds a Ouija session at a ranch where Jesse James used to hang out. He rambles through the Whaley House, where the unfortunate drifter Yankee Jim was badly hanged by an inept hangman, and who is still sore about the whole thing.

That's real ghost huntin'! What I do is just armchair ghost hunting. I paste on my goose pimples. Richard comes by his honestly.

Arthur Myers

(Latest Book, "A Ghost Hunter's Guide")

So You Want to See a Ghost

So you want to see a ghost. You have heard all the stories, read all the books and shuddered at the movies Spielbergian special effects. Now only a real ghost will satisfy your curiosity.

Unfortunately, real ghosts are not as dramatic as those of fiction. Real ghosts appear much like real people. They never carry their heads in their hands or wear sheets. No real ghost would be caught dead rattling chains about. The number of sightings alone is enough to encourage the would be ghost hunter that his quest for a real ghost is not in vain. In 1987, a Roper poll survey indicated that 13% of the American people claimed that they had experienced what they thought was a ghost.

How much of that number was sheer overactive imagination or explainable natural phenomena is unknown. Discounting even half of the sightings still leaves millions of people in the United States who have actually seen a ghost.

Before planning your ghost hunt you must first find a haunted site to investigate. Short of Disneyland, few places advertise themselves as "Haunted Houses." In this instance, looking in the yellow pages is doomed to failure, for there isn't a listing for haunted houses. In seeking places to investigate, several guidelines can be used to narrow your search.

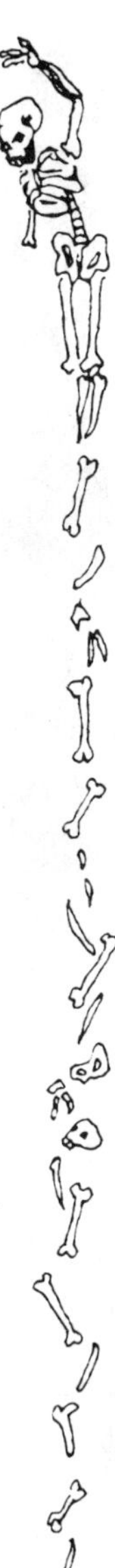

1. Many haunted houses have lurid histories as the sites of murders and suicides. Finding a place with a known history of tragedy is one way to locate a haunting.

2. Many haunted sites are not houses at all. Ghosts can haunt almost any place, building or stretch of road. Some of the most haunted sites are businesses and other establishments.

3. Almost every theater where plays are produced is rumored to harbor spectres. Finding a playhouse without a ghost is difficult!

4. Some lonely roads are known to be haunted by hitchhik-

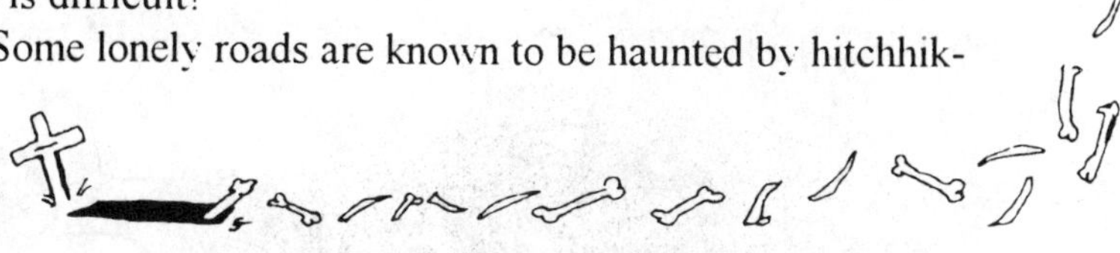

ing phantoms. Highways with a history of accidents and death are singled out as most ghost ridden.

5. Battlefields are also known to hold ghosts. Phantom armies march over some of history's best known battlefields. Fortunately our area has been free of massive armed encounters. History records that San Pasqual, in San Diego County was the scene of a fatal confrontation between Mexican Lancers and Yankee troops in 1847. The dead were buried in a mass grave. Since that time cold winds and strange cries echo through the canyon.

6. Tradition states that cemeteries are good places to look for an occasional spectre. Over the years several cemeteries have gained reputations for having ghosts. Records indicate that few real ghosts haunt cemeteries. Ghosts choose to haunt places where they passed away or lived, rather than their final resting place.

Once you have located a site to investigate, how do you go about it? Clearly ropes and nets are not going to be effective, nor will a glass mason jar hold an active spirit. Still ghosts can be captured, on film, video tape and audio tape. The instances of taking a ghosts picture are rare but it can be accomplished. Experiments in Europe (Mostly in Germany and Great Britain) indicate that haunting ghosts can be video taped. Many times infrared film has been used to photograph ghosts but be very careful because infrared photography is tricky business. Be sure to load the film following all directions, lest your suspected phantom prove to be a simple light leak. Tape recorders have also been used in haunted house investigations with some success. The recorders have gotten odd voices that are not those of the ghost hunting team. These voices are never heard at the time that the recordings are made but turn up mysteriously during playback. They have a low whispering quality and limit themselves to only a few words. This type of phenomenon is known as E.V.P. for Electronic Voice Phenomenon. To attempt to record spirit voices, be sure to use new music quality tapes. Use a quality tape recorder with a remote microphone. It can be left alone in a haunted room as it records, or questions can be asked of

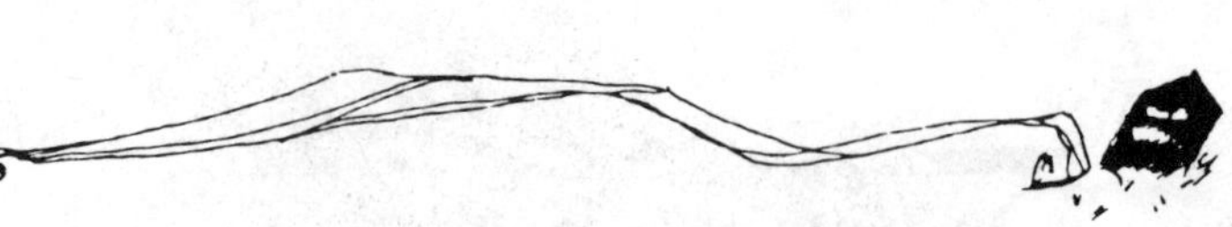

the alleged ghost. During playback there might be detected an answer to a question!

The goal of the ghost hunter should be to prove or disprove the existence of a ghost. To this end the chief goal is to collect data. Psychic researchers should try to interview those who have witnessed the haunting and check their accounts against the known history of the site. Ghost hunters should map the location to accurately plot out any ghostly movements and chart out any areas that seem strangely cold. Cold spots are symptomatic of a haunting. Then, and only then, can you begin the most demanding and most rewarding part of a ghost hunt, the stake out!

The long, all-night wait can be a lonely affair. Be sure to take along a ghost hunter's most valuable tool, a thermos full of hot, black coffee and sandwiches. Always carry a dependable flashlight and wear rubber soled shoes. Be wary of drops in temperature, the air feels cooler just before the materialization of a spirit. Why this odd coldness is present is as yet unknown but has been recorded for thousands of years.

Be sure to take accurate notes about all events; even the most trivial. In such a stake out, those who have psychic gifts can be invaluable in sensing the presence of a ghost. Have cameras ready at all times; ghosts come when they are least expected and sightings often last less than thirty seconds. Patience and perseverance are needed to encounter a fleeting phantom, but with a little luck you may have the chance to be scared out of your wits!

Ghosts have been with Man since the dawn of recorded history, but their true nature is still unknown. Perhaps with research and effort this phenomenon can be explained.

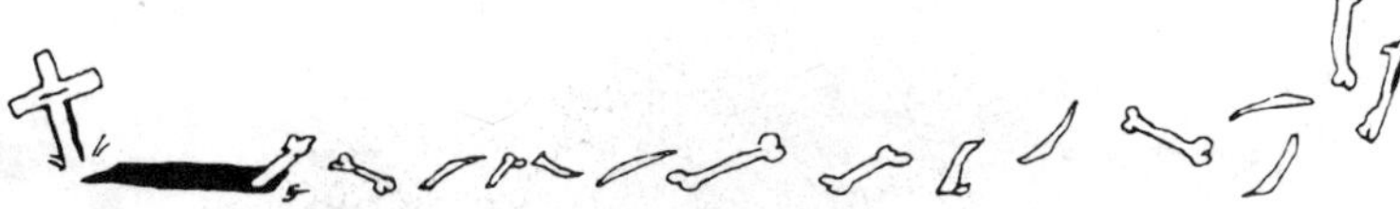

California's Most Haunted House

His face grew red, and he began to visibly shake and gag. Could it be that the psychic researcher was feeling the ever-tightening noose of a hanging that took place in 1852?

Thomas Whaley built his impressive red brick house in Old Town San Diego, in 1856 on, a low hill with a view of the harbor. Mr. Whaley didn't know or didn't care that he was building his mansion on the site of the municipal execution grounds. Almost from the first the house was rumored to be haunted by the ghosts of hanged criminals.

Today the Whaley House has been converted into a museum dedicated to the early pioneers who developed San Diego. The stories of phantoms have continued to circulate. Today the Whaley House is said to be the most haunted house in all of California! Many of the greatest ghost hunters in all of the land have conducted investigations at the historic home, and each one has come away convinced that something mysterious does indeed walk the halls of this building.

"Psychic researchers have informed us that this one is the most actively haunted house in the world," confided the site manager, June Reading, "and they're right!"

Over the last three decades hundreds of visitors have experienced the unknown in this house. They have seen moving shadows, heard laughter and music, observed rocking chairs rock by themselves and felt chilling cold spots.

The writer and parapsychologist Hans Holzer investigated the site and saw a figure at the top of the stairs, a figure he believed was the restless ghost of Thomas Whaley himself. His research team also uncovered evidence of several other phantoms in this old house. At one time a local television crew did a documentary of the place. The host, a very young Regis Philbin, saw a face appear on one of the walls during the taping.

Other ghost hunters who have investigated this one haunting include Susy Smith, noted author on the supernatural, and Antoinette May, psychic researcher and writer. They too

came away convinced that the brick pile was filled with unexplainable phenomena. After reading of these exploits I felt compelled to undertake my own investigation, using people I know and trust. I did not inform the people who manage the Whaley House, I wanted this visit to be a completely random event without possibility of anything preset by the present staff. A team of researchers visited several haunted places in San Diego, with limited reactions. I saved the old Whaley House for last. I kept the group in the dark about this site as much as possible, not wishing to stimulate an overactive imagination into conjuring up a self induced hallucination. The team arrived like regular tourists.

They first went into the court room. Thomas Whaley had rented out part of his house to the local courts as trial space. Many strange things have taken place in that room over the last few years, including visitors seeing a heavy chain swing by itself. I must confess that the moment I stepped into this room I felt a well-defined chill creep up my spine. I watched the chain but it rested, un-moving. The rest of the team began to spread out on their own, in groups of two and three, until I was left in the room quite alone. I was hoping to relax and feel some of the reported supernatural residents of the old place. I didn't get to rest more than a minute or two. One of the team came charging in with wide-eyed fear.

"Mr. Senate, Senate," she said, "you got to see this" She pulled at my arm and jerked me towards the stairway to the second floor. Another member of the team tried to stop us on the way up, claiming that some force had attempted to trip her on the stairs! But the first team member had me firmly by the arm and would not release me.

She pulled me along while the others followed. At the top of the stairs two others were waiting, looking into one of the rooms. They were watching something with hypnotic interest. I was pushed before them, and watched as one of the rocking chairs moved back and forth a few inches. I could detect no wires or strings in the room. A glass pane separated us from the room - a normal thing in a historic house museum filled with valuable antiques - no one was in the room, the windows were closed, yet the chair seemed to be moving.

Another couple came forward, stating that they had seen two small girls in one of the rooms and had watched as the figures vanished away. They were as white as a sheet and shaking from the unexpected encounter with a real phantom." We saw them" the young woman said clutching the arm of her husband, a burly construction worker, "They were just standing there by the window looking out. They were dressed in long white gowns. Like nightgowns." Her husband nodded his head in agreement adding, "They turned and looked at us and then they became transparent and were gone." The couple had joined the group as a lark—the look on their faces indicated that they had really gotten their money's worth. Another team member came running up from the stairway. "There's someone breathing in the Kitchen" she yelled. "There is nothing there but you can hear them clearly." I commented that it might be the ghost of Anna Whaley, the wife of the builder, who died in the house in 1913.

I began to write out their experiences when still another member - a member who identified himself as a complete skeptic - ran up to me red in the face. He told me to come with him on the double. Because of the look on his face, I followed. Gone was the sneer of the non-believer, to be replaced by a look that indicated wonder, and perhaps even a trace of fear. He took me to the archway that lead into the music room, on the first floor, and bid me to stand under the arch.

"What do you feel?" he asked. I didn't feel anything, and told him so. "Did you feel anything around your neck?" he asked. I didn't, and asked what he had experienced. In a disjointed narrative, he explained how he had stood under the arch and felt something tighten around his neck. It had happened twice, each time he stood under the arch. I asked if he would try it once again. He agreed and as he took his place under this arch he gasped and seemed to struggle with something twisting around his neck. I pulled him from the archway as he turned purple. He didn't know the history of

the house. He didn't know the that the archway was built on the exact site of the scaffold used to hang "Yankee" Jim Robinson in 1852 - his crime, stealing a rowboat. The hanging had been a botched job from the start. A drunken hangman had failed to measure Jim's legs and instead of quickly breaking his neck, Jim slowly, painfully strangled to death. The self-proclaimed skeptic had become a believer.

He had come on the ghost hunt only to please his wife and saw it only as a lark - until he felt the rope that took the life of "Yankee" Jim. Over the years more events have been recorded in the historic Whaley House. Though no one encountered the mustachioed man in the dark frock coat, believed by many to be the wandering ghost of Thomas Whaley himself, or smelled his distinctive Havana cigars, the group was convinced that the stories of super- natural goings on were true.

Of the thirteen members of the San Diego investigation, everyone, skeptic as well as believer, experienced something out of the ordinary at the Whaley House. The team concluded that this mansion truly lived up to it's reputation as a real haunted house.

California's Haunted Battlefield

It is a lonely windswept place where native scrub brush and wildlife live much as they have for countless centuries in Southern California. But this hallowed ground is haunted. Here, only 35 miles northeast of San Diego, a battle was fought in a shameful war. Here at San Pasqual one of the last battles of the Mexican-American war was fought between American Dragoons, under General Stephen Kearney, and Lancers, under Mexican General Andres Pico.

Battles leave deep psychic scars upon the land and many accounts exist of ghosts wandering the sites of combat years after the last shot had been fired.

The battle of San Pasqual wasn't a large battle when compared to the battles of the Civil War or even the Revolution but it has the distinction of being the largest battle fought in California. Like many of the haunted battlefields of the world, controversy swirls around the outcome. Who really won the battle? Military historians have debated that question for almost 150 years.

When The United States declared war on the Republic of Mexico, American strategy outlined several offensives on several fronts. One force, designated the Army of the West, started from Fort Levenworth, Kansas, and invaded New Mexico, capturing Sante Fe. After establishing American control with almost no opposition, General Kearney was ordered to march west to assist in capturing California. Forces under the command of John C. Fremont had invaded the state and sent dispatches east informing the war department that California was in American hands. General Kearney of the Army of the West sent most of his troops back to Sante Fe, and proceeded west with only a reduced force into what was thought to be occupied territory.

It is sometimes said that the people of old California were well known for their hospitality, and when they heard that the Yankees wanted a war they, as hospitable people, provided one for them. Yes, California had been captured, but they

quickly rebelled, under the leadership of Mexican General Jose Maria Flores. Los Angeles was retaken, along with every town, village and mission south of Santa Barbara — with the exception of San Diego.

The port city was defended by American gun boats under Commodore Robert F. Stockton, and stood as the last American outpost in all of Southern California. Even the northern half of the state was in an uproar, and several small conflicts were fought. Into this quagmire General Kearney marched his exhausted, bedraggled dragoons. Once in California, Commodore Stockton reinforced the remains of the Army of the West with 35 marines and sent word that a force of California Militia Lancers was encamped at the Indian village of San Pasqual. As the sun came up on the morning of December 6th, 1846, Kearney's forces slowly advanced upon the enemy. They had hoped to surprise the caballeros as they slept but, unknown to the invaders, they had been under observation for several days. General Andres Pico, the leader of the Militia Lancers and brother of California governor Pio Pico, knew about the attack and was ready for it.

The battle lasted only for a few minutes, but what it lacked in time it made up in violence and intensity. The well-mounted lancers fell upon the American forces from all sides with eleven-foot lances and swords. In the rain and mist the encounter degenerated into dozens of small hand-to-hand skirmishes. One California lancer, formerly a dim-witted cowhand and the butt of many jokes, transformed into a wild man. On the battlefield he won his nickname "El Lobo," the wolf. Time and time again he led the charge against the enemy. When his lance splintered, he took a sword from a fallen comrade, using it until it broke in two. Finally he wielded a rusty ax until he was clubbed down by a Yankee musket stock. For years the old Vaqueros in Southern California would whisper, "If we had a dozen more like 'El Lobo' we would have pushed the Yankees into the sea."

General Kearney was lanced in the arm during the battle, and the American artillery piece was captured and carried away by cheering Californios. The Americans remained on the field as the lancers withdrew, but they had taken 40% casualties and were unable to pursue the enemy.

The Californios, as ill-trained militia, were unable to finish off the invaders once and for all. Pico did launch a second attack five days later, and this too was driven off after the Americans took more casualties. A rescue column reached Kearney's force on December 11, and escorted them into the safety of San Diego.

The Battle of San Pasqual stood as a draw, but historians agree that both sides exhibited bravery and determination in their cause. It was this heroism that led to the battlefield site becoming a state park with a walking tour and a small museum outlining the almost forgotten battle. The museum and tour are interesting and accurate in the historical details of the battle, but they do not tell of the folklore of this place.

The tour maps do not show where ghosts ride on the night of December 6th, they do not tell of the phantom screams and blasts of icy cold that seem to hover around the place where "El Lobo" fell. The old battleground has long been regarded as haunted by the old timers who tell of seeing phantom lancers and ghostly dragoons locked in eternal combat. The most often told tale is that of Don Leandro Osuna and his huge bay 'El Apache.' It seems that Don Leandro, a wealthy land owner, had joined the local militia to impress a pretty young girl; he had not joined to fight. When the battle began, he tossed away his lance and retreated back to the comforts of his home. In the battle a close friend was killed, and guilt followed the man for the rest of his life. It is said that as he grew older he became bitter and was a hard taskmaster to his Indian workers on his vast Rancho San Dieguito. His out-rages became so terrible that the Natives visited a powerful medicine man, and from him they purchased a powerful poison. During one of Don Leonardo's drunken dinners, they slipped the toxin into his food. His taste buds, numbed by wine and brandy, he consumed the poison without noticing the bitter aftertaste. The next morning he began to feel the pain of the slow acting poison. With awful grin; the Indian

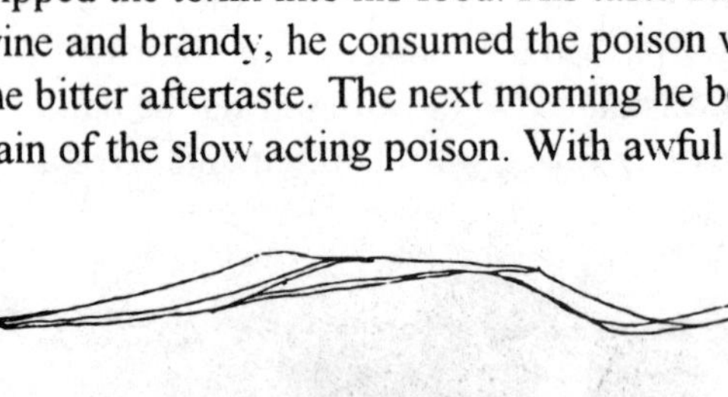

servants told him of the potion. Knowing his painful end would take many days Don Leandro took his pistol and, pointing the weapon to his temple, he ended his life. As his dying wish to the angels, he re-fights the battle he had fled from in life — doomed to ride with the phantom lancers until the end of the world.

San Pasqual Battlefield Park is indeed a strange, mysterious place where memories seem to linger of a half-forgotten war and forgotten men who battled so long ago. Those who have reported ghostly manifestations seem to agree that the most active time is early December — in the late afternoon, just before the sun sets.

Ghosts of the Gonzales Adobe

The psychic researcher paused, closely, meticulously examining the photograph as it developed in his hands. Could it be that his instant camera had captured the faces of phantom children looking down from the second floor of the historic adobe? If he had, it would not be the first time this had occurred, and perhaps it would not be the last.

The 1879 adobe home of Temecula pioneer Jose Maria Gonzales is, strangely enough, surrounded by a modern shopping mall! The modern buildings, in keeping with the style of the older building, have a Spanish - Mediterranean look. The adobe has been preserved and restored and today it is a flower shop called "The Ivy Cottage." Over the years the old Gonzales Adobe has gained the reputation as being haunted.

The first accounts date back to one of the last families to live in the house. They reported numerous poltergeist-like events in the early 1970's. They woke to find the kitchen utensils scattered about on the floor. Once the mother of the family was given a sharp push by an unseen hand as she descended a flight of stairs. It was as if someone or something was trying to push her down the narrow stairs!

During the conversion of the 1,078 square foot adobe into 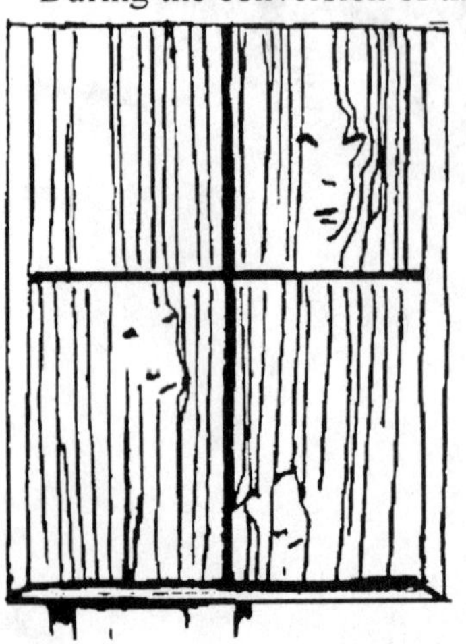 space for a shop, several of the construction workers were spooked by ghostly voices that seemed to come out of thin air. That was before a local photographer claimed to have taken pictures of the historic residence only to discover phantom faces of small children looking down from the second story window — while the building was unoccupied.

It was these accounts that lured local psychic researcher Brian Black to the community of Temecula in search of the ghosts of the Gonzales Adobe. He found the site with little trouble in the old Adobe Plaza located on the corner of Overland Drive and Jefferson Avenue. Mr. Black found that the adobe didn't look old at all. It had been modernized to a point where only it's thick walls betrayed the adobe construction of the building.

He asked the shop owner about the ghostly manifestations said to hover near the place but, though he knew all the lurid stories, the owner confessed that in all the years he had been at this shop he hadn't seen or heard a thing. Mr. Black questioned people who came into the business and was told that, though everyone had heard the building was haunted, none could give the name of an eyewitness. It seemed that everyone had heard the story second or third hand. Black then secured permission to tour the upstairs that seemed to be the center of the psychic disturbances.

He found it a dark and spooky place, now just used for storage. Still, the feeling was peaceful and calm. It didn't feel haunted at all. Mr. Black took numerous photographs, using an instant camera, in hopes of snapping a picture of the phantom. His pictures documented his visit to the legendary haunted house of Temecula. He took several pictures of the second floor from outside. It was then that one of the photographs seemed to show something out of the ordinary. As the picture developed, several hazy outlines seemed to take shape on the glass of the window — they did resemble faces. More photographs were taken but no other images were found.

Mr. Black had the original photograph blown up in hopes of making the images sharper, but it only caused the faint outlines to vanish. Were the pictures reflections or flaws in the film? Could it be the ghostly children or wishful thinking? Is the old Gonzales Adobe really haunted? As the Spanish say, "Quien Sabe?", who knows?

The Ghosts of Capistrano

The huge trunk of the ancient pepper tree looms before the 1794 Rios Adobe in San Juan Capistrano. This is the very center of the most haunted neighborhood in the United States!

Beneath the gnarled trunk, the legendary White Lady of Capistrano is seen. She has continued to prowl Los Rios Street, at the corner of Verdugo and Los Rios, near the old pepper tree for over a hundred years! Local residents, many descendants of the original Spanish settlers, claim that she is only one of five "white ladies" rumored to haunt the mission community of San Juan Capistrano, in Orange County.

But the white lady of Los Rios is believed to be the most fearful of the terrible five, for she comes complete with a terrifying pet; a hellish hound that spits fire and brimstone, a beast that she keeps loosely under her control with a long rawhide leash. Some say that the lady wears a long wedding gown and has a skull-like face. One young man who encountered the Los Rios lady claimed he saw her three times on his way home from a dance. She seemed to be ahead of him even though she never moved! When he ran home and dashed into his house, his father, a long time resident, told him that the White Lady had been seen for decades and, though she had a fearsome appearance, "she never hurts anyone." There are other ladies in white. One, The Del Obispo White Lady, is said to lead lucky people to where gold is buried. Still another haunt, another lady in a long white dress, is chained to the narrow strip of land near the railroad tracks. She is a young lady who is believed to have taken poison and placed herself on the railway to commit suicide. The comely lady now haunts the site of her desperate act, a filmy misty creature with icy breath. Several of the adobe buildings in Capistrano are said to harbor haunts. The Rios Adobe, still owned by the Rios family, is haunted by the spirits of all those who have visited the house in its two hundred years of history. One of the Rios's sons recently heard boots walking through the halls. Fearing an intruder, he took his pistol and searched the place. He found the adobe empty and the doors and windows locked on the inside! He asked family members of the incident and discovered that they too had heard mysterious footsteps. Some think they may be footsteps of the celebrated bandit, Joaquin Murietta. Legend holds that the outlaw, a friend of Gregario Rios, would spend the night hiding in the attic room of the old adobe while lawmen searched the area. He would always leave the next morning, but conveniently leave behind a small bag of gold coins to compensate for his stay. Perhaps it is his hurried footsteps that echo across time and space through the halls of the Rios Adobe?

Not far from the Rios Adobe stands the Montanez Adobe. It too was built in 1794. It too has attracted a number of ghostly tales. Today, the small two room adobe has been turned into a museum. From time to time visitors tell of hearing chanting voices and seeing a glowing ball of light in the corner of the main room or sala. Psychic Debbie Christenson Senate felt a woman's presence in the small adobe when she felt the door.

Having heard many psychic stories of ghosts in San Juan Capistrano, a group of psychic researchers boarded the train and rode to the picturesque mission town to walk the narrow streets of the Los Rios neighborhood in search of its many phantoms. They found the trees twisted and photogenic, but lacking in white ladies. They were on the lookout for demon dogs, but the only canines they encountered were of the normal, non fire-spitting kind. It was at the historic Montanez Adobe that they began to feel the journey might not have been in vain. There was a distinct atmosphere that hovered near the small building. Mr. Ken Christenson, a member of the team placed his head near the ancient adobe wall and for a brief moment, saw an image of a religious statue. It seemed to be a winged figure, perhaps an angel. But the location where he saw the form didn't conform to the reported location of the small chapel, once part of the building. Research on the Montanez adobe uncovered that the Adobe chapel was not on the north side of the house but on the rear porch! The psychic impression had proved superior to the historical record!

The group next walked to the El Adobe Restaurant on El Camino Capistrano. Formerly two adobes, the Mexican restaurant has been a favorite of movie stars and presidents. One half of the El Adobe was once the Juzagado Adobe. Used as a court room, it came complete with a dungeon. They have converted the icy cold jail cell into a wine cellar. Waiters in the restaurant complain that, when they go into the dungeon, they feel watched by unseen eyes. The group was invited to tour the wine cellar, and more than one set of goose pimples rose up upon entering the chilling atmosphere of the small chamber.

The tour of San Juan Capistrano confirmed there are ghosts in the mission town. The stories, though mostly folklore, are firmly rooted in real psychic encounters. The mission San Juan Capistrano has long been rumored to hold its share of spectres. The ghost of an Indian woman named 'Magdalena' is said to wander the grounds of the mission holding a single candle. She died clutching the candle on December 8, 1812, when a massive earthquake toppled the stone church, killing 40 mission Indians. They say her face is seen in one of the upper windows of the ruined church. Another story tells of a strange blue light in the mission cemetery. A few years ago a psychic research team placed a tape recorder on one of the graves and, when the tape was played back, there was a sad voice saying; " I'm scared," and "I'm cold." The words were in English, even though the graves were of Spanish and Indian-speaking natives attached to the Mission. Perhaps with research and other investigations a true listing of Capistrano's many phantoms can someday be made.

The Ghosts of Calico

What better place to search for ghosts than a ghost town? It was that rationale that motivated our investigation of the ghost town of Calico, located nine miles east of Barstow on Highway 91. The psychic search turned up several colorful spectres.

The town was founded in 1881, and named for the colorful rock cliffs that surround the town. In the years before World War I, over 13 million dollars worth of silver ore was extracted from her mines. But, with the decline of silver prices, Calico slowly became a classic "ghost town."

Today the ruined buildings have been restored and are open as historical attractions. The dirt streets have been paved and costumed actors walk the board sidewalks holding mock gun fights for the camera snapping tourists. Our group discovered that there is much more to Calico than Western-style buildings and curio shops; there is a psychic Calico undreamed of by tourists.

For years rumors have circulated that ghosts wandered the historic ghost town. A number of psychics visiting the community reported odd feelings and strange phenomena. Research uncovered a local legend of a ghost that dated back to the days of the silver boom. A man named McIntrye was crushed in a cave-in. His body was never found, and was left entombed in the lower levels of the mine shaft. From that day on many claim to hear his desperate voice echoing from the mine. He is described as calling for help and then lapsing into heart rendering sobs. After the fatal accident, many miners refused to work in that shaft, fearing what came to be known as "the old spook."

Finding the exact location of this mine proved difficult. A number of shafts dot the landscape. But, with some questioning, our team was given directions to the site a quarter of a mile out of town. After a difficult hike in the heat of the noonday sun, we climbed to a yawning pit we believed to be the correct mine. Before the stark shaft were piles of discolored earth. These were the "tailings," or discarded material from the digging of the mine. We had been warned to keep out of the mine shaft itself. The aging supports could give away at any time. We did not wish to join the ghost of McIntyre in his lonely vigil, so we simply called down the dark shaft. No sound answered our cries. One of our group, a gifted psychic, went into a trance-like state in an attempt to communicate with the trapped spectre of the long dead miner. Her eyes flickered under the glare of the bright sun. After a time in meditation, she smiled.

"He's gone now," she said softly. "He has at last found peace and forgiveness. He blamed someone for the accident. I think it was one of the owners of the mine he felt was responsible for his death." The psychic looked up for a long moment before she continued.

"He has moved on. His name was James, James McIntrye. He was a Roman Catholic in his youth. He wanted a proper Mass and burial."

Finding that the phantom had found his final reward, we walked to the town and purchased soft drinks. We had more luck in our ghost hunt touring the two dozen buildings that make up Calico. Only four of the structures are original, the rest reconstructions. The team felt nothing odd or strange in the new buildings. One member characterized them as "just normal." They were in marked contrast to the older structures. The old Lane's General Store seemed charged with psychic energy. Our psychic became excited upon entering the adobe store.

"I see a woman," she stammered, looking into an empty corner. "She was a strong woman; she is wearing a hat. It's like a cowboy hat, yes . . . it's a man's hat. She is very happy with what they have done with the store."

I asked one of the clerks if she believes the place was haunted. The lady smiled in a tolerant way that betrayed that I was not the first one to ask such a question. "A lot of strange things have happened here," she confided. "You know, doors opening, things moving. Mostly just sounds. Well, like people walking around. People come in and say

that they feel things in here, like places that are cold. Two people even said they saw a shape like a woman. I have been here a long time and I never seen a thing like that. But, it can get really spooky in here sometimes. The ghost might be Lucy Lane, who operated the store during the years when Calico was a real ghost town slowly dying under the desert sun."

Walking the streets, we entered the Old Maggie Mine. This silver mine, located in the center of town, is open to the public for a small fee. Having been cheated out of seeing the inside of the last mine shaft, we elected to tour the inside of the Maggie Mine in the hope of scaring up a phantom. The coolness of the underground mine was in stark contrast to the heat on the surface. The tunnel seemed to reek of foreboding. Our psychic had been reluctant to enter but, once inside, she became enthusiastic. "Chinese!" she explained feeling the rock walls. "There were lots of Chinese here. They were so sad. This was not a safe mine." The psychic moved ahead of us, almost running. We caught up to her staring into a small room cut out of the rock. "Chang," she murmured. "A man named Chang died in there. It was not an accident, it was from illness, something in this chest. He wanted to return to his village in China. He was trying to save enough money to buy a grave in his home town. But the coughing sickness came to him one winter and he had to spend his cash on doctors. He spent all he saved and then died. He is buried here on 'Boot Hill'... He needs to realize that he can leave anytime he wants." She moved on after saying a short prayer for the long dead Chinese miner. When we returned to the surface, I was surprised to find the psychic covered with perspiration and shaking like a leaf.

The ghosts of Calico reflect the lusty history of this mining town. They seem like memories frozen in time and space. A tour of the town, in the right frame of mind, is like stepping back into another world.

The Ghosts of the Long Beach Adobe

The two story adobe at historic Rancho Los Cerritos has been preserved as a historic landmark of California's past. Built in 1844 by American merchant, Jonathan Temple, it is one of the best examples of its kind of construction in Southern California. The old adobe is haunted by as many as four distinct ghosts!

Decades ago the grave of Jonathan Temple was moved. Its lonely location was in the way of a modern freeway. Some believe that is why the phantom has taken up permanent residence in his former home. In life Don Juan Temple, as the locals called him, was known as a hospitable man, and so it seems he continues this in death, for they have seen him in the company of other ghosts. One witness saw what was thought to be Temple with two children. They might be his daughters who are buried on the ranch. For decades reports of lights going on and off by themselves have been whispered about the old place. Some people at the old adobe late in the evening reported hearing the distinct sound of bells; lots of small bells. The rancho was, at one point of its history, a vast sheep ranch with over 30,000 sheep. The bells could have been sheep bells. They checked for the origins of the sound and found nothing that could produce such a noise. The former caretaker reported that, when he moved there in the mid-1970's, all sorts of things began to happen. He was in the place by himself, and each sound seemed to point to something supernatural. Late in the night he heard the slow pacing of a man wearing heavy boots in the hallway. When he got up to see who it was he found the adobe deserted with all the doors bolted tight. Then the lights began to flicker on and off. Was it bad wiring or could it have been something else?

Several psychics visiting the house were so badly shaken that they refused to set foot in the place again. Some have felt that a fourth spirit wanders the house. It is described as an evil force, bent on frightening people. It is thought to be the

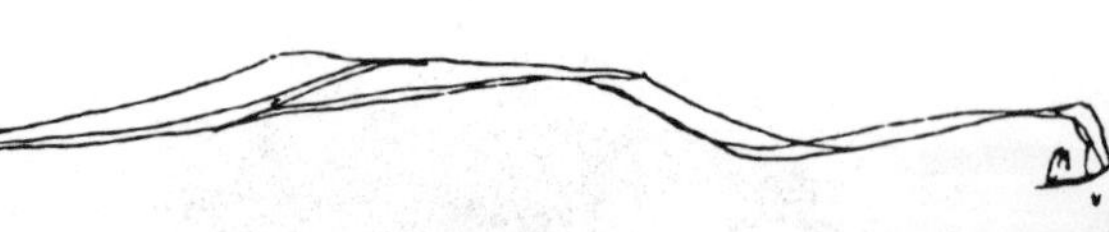

ghost of an ex-foreman who was so bad that the family was scared of him.

Because of the reported psychic disturbances in the house, a seance was held years ago. The director, staff, and a reporter were present when a medium attempted to communicate with the forces that inhabit the adobe. Ten people gathered around a thick library table. Both believers and skeptics felt the heavy table rise off the floor. The director, who didn't believe in ghosts, said something in a mocking tone and the huge table shifted to one side and pinned him against the wall. The reporter wrote in the local newspaper that he had . . . "witnessed a table move in such a strange way that obviously a mystic force was at work." The director never again mocked the ghosts of the Cerritos Adobe — he was sure something out of the ordinary inhabited the place.

The present museum staff report no ghostly manifestation at the historic home, and blame the ghost stories on former caretakers with "vivid imaginations."

The look on the former director when he told of his encounter with the moving table was convincing. His experience wasn't a case of an overactive imagination.

The Rancho Los Cerritos Adobe is located at 4600 Virginia Road, Long Beach, and is open Wednesday through Sunday from one to five. If you believe yourself to have some psychic ability, tour the historic adobe and see if you feel the sudden dramatic drop in temperature that is the first sign that a ghost is about to materialize. Perhaps you too could visit the gracious spirit of "Don Juan" Temple and his daughters, or encounter the icy cold of the ex-foreman, or maybe just hear the tinkle of the sheep bells. As you enter the grounds of the adobe pause for a moment and think back to the days when this was the busy ranch house of a vast sheep ranch where fiestas would last for days on end. Perhaps those days are not over and the ghosts stay on to continue their carefree lifestyle.

Ghosts of the RMS Queen Mary

The great passenger liner, RMS Queen Mary, is now docked at pier "J" in Long Beach, California. Her sailing days are over and she rests out her twilight years as a floating hotel and tourist attraction. But her rest is not an easy one, for many report restless spirits wandering her decks and spectral sounds echoing down her companionways.

The huge liner began at Clydebank, Scotland, where the keel was laid in December 1930. Her construction was marred by delays and accidents. At last the British government was forced to loan the company nine and a half million pounds to finish the ship. The RMS Queen Mary sailed on her maiden voyage, May 27, 1936. She reached New York in four days, fifteen hours and received a thunderous welcome, with a parade of water-spouting fire boats escorting her up the Hudson River. The Queen Mary became the rage of the smart set. Actors and actresses, statesmen and royalty sought out the ship. Parties on the Queen Mary could last the entire length of the voyage, proving that "getting there was indeed half the fun."

Even to this day the security personnel on board the ship report the sounds of phantom voices, clinking glasses and laughter, the ghosts of the decadent days when starlets and comics crossed the oceans in lavish style. The security people have also observed "a woman in white." She is a young woman in a white backless evening gown of the late 1930's. She coyly walks with a swaying motion to the art deco lounge and drapes herself over the piano and vanishes. Perhaps she is a long dead debutante who dreamed of a Hollywood career.

In 1939, the British government requisitioned the ship for use as a troop transport. A terrible riot took place on the overcrowded vessel. The brawl grew so violent that the captain called an escort warship for help in combating what might have become a mutiny. Before marines could stop the riot, a kitchen cook was pushed into a blazing oven and burned to death. Since then dishes have been moved mysteri-

ously and lights have gone on and off by themselves.

The RMS Queen Mary resumed passenger service in 1947. The luxurious liner held her own for a few years until low airfares and jet aircraft began to take their toll on the passenger trade. Because the ship was losing money at a rate of over three million pounds per year, the Queen Mary was sold to the city of Long Beach in 1967. Since the conversion of the craft to a floating hotel, guards have reported many strange events aboard the ship.

Several tell of encountering a girl wearing a green miniskirt walking near the ship's indoor pool. The apparition suddenly vanishes behind a pillar. Others report seeing a woman swimming in the pool, only to discover the image mysteriously gone. Ship's records do indeed confirm that a young woman did indeed drown in the swimming pool once. One guard reported that she saw a woman dive into the pool only to find the pool empty. Other personnel have encountered a persistent phantom in the engine rooms at the stern of the vessel. The image is seen in the area known as "shaft alley," where the massive propeller shafts were once monitored. The ghost is seen wearing white coveralls and seems involved with repairing the ship. The guards refer to this spectre as "Jonathan."

For these reasons a ghost hunt and seance was held on board the ship. Debbie Christenson Senate toured the haunted swimming pool and was stunned to see a red glow in one of the dressing rooms and a figure swimming under the water. The image didn't last long and others saw bubbles appear in the pool's water even though there wasn't any reason why the bubbles should be there. Debbie agreed to act as medium as we gathered at midnight to attempt spirit communication. We held hands tightly in the dim light of the chamber as the medium slumped forward in her chair. For several long moments she breathed deeply, going deeper into a trance. The woman began to moan in a deep voice. It was a moan of pain and suffering. I was leading the seance.

Debbie sat up in her chair, her eyes still closed, her face twisted in pain.

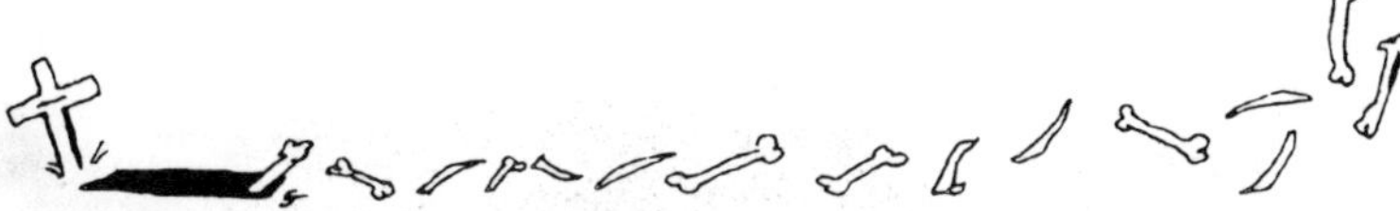

(Debbie): "My legs," she cried out. "My legs. Pain."

(Richard): "What is the matter with your legs?"

(Debbie): "Pain. My legs are wounded."

(Richard): "What is your name?"

(Debbie): "Carlo."

(Richard): "Did you have another name?"

(Debbie): "Carlo Giovetti," she answered in a pained voice.

(Richard): "Are you Italian?"

(Debbie): "Si."

(Richard): "How were your legs injured?"

(Debbie): "Shot down, crashed."

(Richard): "Who shot you down?"

(Debbie): "English," she said with a sneer of hate, English Spitfires."

(Richard): "What year is this?"

(Debbie): "1941."

(Richard): "What did you do?"

(Debbie): "Pilot, Regia Aeronotica."

(Group member): "What kind of plane did you fly?"

(Debbie): "Falco, Falco, CR 42 Falco."

(Richard): "What was this plane like?"

(Debbie): "Biplane. Falco is a good plane."

(Richard): "Biplanes were not used that late. Are you sure it was a biplane, two wings?"

(Debbie): "Si, Falco."

(Richard): "Where were you based?"

(Debbie): "Bengali, Bengali."

(Group member): "Is that in North Africa?"

(Debbie): "Si."

(Richard): "How did you get to North Africa?"

(Debbie): "Kangaroo, I was kangarooed."

(Richard): "What is a kangaroo? Was that the name of a ship?"

(Debbie): "Airplane, Kangaroo, Falco folded up. Placed in Kangaroo. My plane folded up."

(Richard): "Did you mean your Falco folded up and crashed?"

(Debbie): "No, no, Kangarooed. SM 82, flown to Bengali."

(Richard): "What is a Kangaroo?" I asked for a second time.

(Debbie): "Plane, three-motored transport."

(Group member) "Your plane was folded up inside another larger plane and flown to North Africa?"

(Debbie): "Si."

(Richard): "What was your squadron number?"

(Debbie): "162-B, no 162-A."

(Richard): "What were you doing the day you were shot down?"

(Debbie): "Reconnaissance over Bar Dee Ah."

(Richard): "What happened after you were shot down?"

(Debbie): "Captured by British, Taken to Alexandria."

(Richard): "What happened then, did the English take care of your legs?"

(Debbie): "No, British kicked me. Placed on board the Queen Mary."

(Richard): "Where were you placed?"

(Debbie): "In the bottom of the ship. The air was hot, so hot."

(Richard): "Did you see a doctor?"

(Debbie): "The English want to cut off my legs! I won't let them. Bugs are crawling all over my legs. Make them stop!"

(Richard): "Why do they want to amputate your legs?"

(Debbie): "I will never fly again. Don't let them cut off my legs!"

(Richard): "What is it like on the ship?"

(Debbie): "Infantry—infantry. They placed me with infantry men, pigs!"

(Richard): "Where were they taking you?"

(Debbie): "Australia."

(Richard): "Were there any injured men on this ship?"

(Debbie): "Many, five or six died each day. It was so hot."

(Richard): "What did they do with the dead?"

(Debbie): "Overboard."

(Richard): "Was there a priest on board? Someone to

confide in. For last rites?"

(Debbie): "No priest. My legs hurt so bad. I can't feel them now. O mama! O mama!"

(Richard): "What's happening now?"

(Debbie): "They put me in a bag, a canvas bag. It's cold, the water is so cold."

The medium let out a scream and fell forward in her chair. Several other personalities came through the medium as the seance continued, but none revealed the amount of information that "Carlo" did.

Later investigations confirmed that the Italian air force did use a biplane fighter, the fiat CR 42, code named Falco, during the second World War. They were used in fighting around the city of Bangazi. It is known that prisoners of war were transported on the Queen Mary, but later in the war.

So far, research has failed to uncover a pilot named Carlo Giovetti, or a type of plane called a "Kangaroo." But, if the account is true, it would reveal mistreatment on the part of the British toward their Italian prisoners of war.

The seance indicates that a number of spirits do indeed wander the decks of the RMS Queen Mary. Later that night, troubled by a violent headache brought on by the long seance, Debbie and I walked the darkened decks of the moored ocean liner. It was almost four a.m. and there wasn't a soul around. We heard footsteps on the deck above us. Debbie turned to me and said, "Those footsteps are made by ghosts!" They seemed so real I doubted this and, as we were close to a stairway I leaped up the steps to confront our fellow night owls—there was no one there as far as I could see.

Ghosts Haunt Civil War Fort

Mr. Fred Duran's job as an exterminator for the County of Los Angeles took him to the very threshold of the unknown. He was visiting the historic Drum Barracks in Wilmington. He was spraying under the sink in the kitchen when he heard footsteps approach. He looked up and saw a tall man wearing clothing from the time of the Civil War. The man was carrying an empty pitcher. In a gravelly voice he said, "I want some water." The exterminator thought the man must be the caretaker of the old barracks who, taking his job seriously, dressed in period clothing. The figure then asked "Have you seen Maria?" When the exterminator continued his work, the man vanished. He felt the stranger simply had left the room silently. After finishing his work, he commented on the dedication of the caretaker with the members of the staff. He was shocked to discover that the caretaker didn't wear costumes — nor did he resemble the man he had seen. In fact that day no one was in period dress. The exterminator had carried on a conversation with a phantom! Upon learning this, Mr. Duran quickly downed three cups of coffee. His sighting of a ghost was only one of many recorded at the historic Drum Barracks. The caretaker, Forest Neil, heard the distinct sounds of footsteps one quiet Monday in 1989. Thinking that intruders may have somehow gotten into the museum when it was not open to the public, he looked down from the stairs on the second floor and saw the door going into what is now the gift shop slowly close by itself. Investigating, he found that he was alone and none of the doors were unlocked!

"I don't call them ghosts," confesses Marge O'Brien, the director of the museum. "We call them spirits."

She first learned of the ghosts in 1986, when she took over the small museum. The former director and caretaker gave her a thick, handwritten volume. In it he had recorded almost twenty years of mysterious events in the building. "Anytime he had an interaction with a spirit he wrote it down at that minute and dated it," recalled Mrs. O'Brien, "It was a real tome. It was strange." This record stimulated her interest in the idea that the old building might be haunted. In doing research on the structure, she began to ask people if any strange things had ever happened in the building. She was surprised at the number of individuals who had experienced ghostly events at the Civil War Era fort.

She interviewed one man who had been born in the building when it was a residence in 1904. He had told her that he had two friends while he lived in the house — two adults that told him strange stories and proved ever present playmates. It was only when he became an adult that he learned his friends were spirits! Mrs. O'Brien interviewed people who grew up in the house across the street. One family recalled seeing a man and a woman walking arm in arm on the balcony of the Drum Barracks at a time when it was dark and abandoned.

At this time Mrs. O'Brien began to notice strange occurrences in the 132-year old building. Lights were turned on in closed rooms. Window shades were raised at night when the building was secured for the night.

The building is the last standing structure of a 60-acre training and supply base that supported troops throughout the Southwest. Over 17,000 troops went through the base to serve the Union cause. Today the building is used as a museum dedicated to California's role in the Civil War.

A well-known psychic, Ms. Barbara Connors, was called in and confirmed that the place is indeed well haunted. She detected Indian spirits in the front of the building. Later O'Brien found in obscure records that a small detachment of Apache scouts was based near there. The psychic told of a man's spirit in the parlor, a man with an injured foot who wanted to stay near the fire. It was later learned that an officer named James Freeman Curtis had lost a foot to frostbite and walked with a limp. Because of the frostbite he always wanted to be warm. The psychic confirmed that a woman's spirit also inhabited the house — a woman named Maria. She went on to say that a young boy also haunts the structure — bouncing a ball on the second floor. The psychic

didn't know about the sounds reported in the building, sounds that were much like those produced by a bouncing ball!

Other psychics and psychic research groups have investigated the old fort and confirmed that at least three ghosts inhabit the place. An officer with a bad leg, a woman named Maria and a little boy. It is thought that the exterminator encountered the officer that day when he spoke to the ghost in the kitchen.

The fort is indeed a mysterious place, and rich in history. If you have an interest in the supernatural and in the history of California in the Civil War, The Drum Barracks is the place to visit.

Abbot Kinney Haunts Venice

They were walking home that night. It wasn't late, and they had not been drinking when they saw the apparition. They were crossing one of the many bridges that cross the canals of Venice, the canals that give the beach community its distinctive flavor. It was a dark night when the two saw coming toward them what appeared to be two large black dogs. They looked like they were running side by side. As they approached, another thing appeared; a top hat, floating in the air five feet above the "dogs." As the image drew closer, the witnesses observed that what they thought were two dogs were two tall boots! A cape appeared, a vest, and as the phantom slowly materialized, they saw it was a man with a cane. He was dressed as if he was going to the opera! They watched as the figure walked passed them on the other side of the bridge. As he continued to walk away, they watched as the cane, the cape, the clothing and the hat vanished, leaving only the boots to walk into the darkness of the night.

Who is the well-dressed ghost that walks the canals of Venice? It is believed to be the restless phantom of Venice builder and dreamer, Abbot Kinney.

In the first years of the Twentieth Century wealthy real estate developer and cigarette king Abbot Kinney planned his ultimate fantasy — to build his own version of Venice, Italy, on the marshlands south of Santa Monica. He had engineers design a system of canals to carry away the water and the team of architects to design the ornate chain of buildings — exotic hotels, pavilions, restaurants, bath houses and businesses. He even built a 1600 foot pier for fishing and strolling, then a popular form of entertainment at the turn of the century.

The new Venice opened on the Fourth of July, 1905. Gondolas and singing gondoliers drifted down the canals and, for a time, it was believed that the California Venice would indeed become the cultural center of Southern California. But, by the 1920's, the dream of Abbot Kinney had faded away and Venice quickly just became another beachside community.

There was a time when Venice was used by the greats of silent Hollywood — Chaplin relaxed at the Waldorf Hotel, Rudolph Valentino danced at the St. Mark's Hotel, Douglas Fairbanks ate ice cream cones on the ocean front walk, and Marion Davies — actress and mistress to William Randolph Hearst enjoyed hot dogs on the pier, Carole Lombard rode the rollercoaster with Claudette Colbert. Venice was the Disneyland of the day. In 1925 the faltering community was incorporated into the City of Los Angeles. The last mayor of Venice, Thomas H. Thurlow, admitted with 20/20 hindsight that joining the City of Los Angeles was a mistake. "We committed suicide," he commented. "That's what we called it and that's what it was." Los Angeles filled in many of the canals, built roads and opened the community to oil developers. Venice became nothing more than an industrial park. The dream was killed by neglect and the rush to exploit oil reserves discovered in the beach community. The ghost of Abbot Kinney has reason to walk the night. His shade has reason to inspect the city he planned and reason to be angry that what should have been a California jewel became a soiled suburb of the urban sprawl of Los Angeles. Perhaps, as the community is restored and Venice becomes an artist's colony, another of Kinney's dreams, his ghost will at last rest in peace.

Hollywood's Haunted Hotel

The trumpet moved. There was no getting around that, it now rested upon the carpeted floor several feet from where it had been placed. This might not have been important except that this was the Montgomery Clift room of the posh Hollywood Roosevelt Hotel, long rumored haunted by a trumpet playing phantom!

The team of ghost hunters had checked into the opulent hotel seeking the wandering ghosts of actors Montgomery Clift and Marilyn Monroe. The goal of the psychic investigation was to confirm the existence of ghosts within the famed hotel.

If phantoms did indeed haunt, they certainly exhibited good taste. A party was held for the office of the Los Angeles District Attorney several years ago in the hotel. The celebration lasted well into the night and as it was winding down, a man and his wife were walking around the mezzanine examining the collection of old pictures on the walls. They saw a man with white hair sitting at the piano near the door to the balcony of the main ballroom. The couple were watching him as they strolled closer. As they drew near the man simply vanished! Shaken, the couple quickly ran down to the front desk to report what they had seen. Oddly enough, the very next day an engineer finishing a project on the third floor saw a man standing in the hall. The man was wearing a white suite and was looking from side to side. The engineer, thinking it was a confused guest, approached him and asked if he could help. The man didn't say a word, he turned and walked down the hall with his hands at his side, toward the fire door at the end of the hall. When the man reached the door he went right though the door without opening it! The stunned engineer could not move from the spot for what seemed like five minutes. Then he ran to report the event to his supervisor.

The hotel Roosevelt is restored to it's original grandeur, when it was the foremost hostelry in the movie capital. Here,

in the hotel's Spanish style grand ballroom the very first Academy Awards were given out in 1927. One of the first targets selected for the Hollywood ghost hunts was the persistent cold spot reported in the grand ballroom. The workers in the hotel have long argued that a spot in the room seemed strangely charged with an icy coldness. The team spread out like blind men, arms outstretched, seeking some impression of coldness. They were rewarded when the spot was located. It seemed to be a distinct column of cold. There were no vents or air-conditioning elements to explain away the phenomenon. Something was detectable in that one place near the center of the room. It was measured at almost three feet in diameter and at least six feet in height. Psychic Debbie Christenson Senate felt the presence of a young man in the cold spot. The floor was checked to determine if there was some type of refrigeration unit beneath the floorboards that would explain the icy coldness. None was detected. The management of the hotel had examined every conceivable explanation in an attempt to find an answer to this riddle. Members of the team returned to the ballroom later in the evening and determined the spot had not moved, and was, if anything colder. Perhaps the coldness is linked to someone who lost in the competition for the first Oscar?

Next the team examined a long mirror rumored to be haunted by the ghost of sex goddess Marilyn Monroe. We were told by the management that the mirror had been the property of the late star, and reports of a sighting of the blond movie star are true. A maid, cleaning the mirror, had seen the misty figure of Miss Monroe standing behind her. The maid turned to see nothing. Several strange events had occurred when a documentary team had attempted to reenact this event for a Halloween special in 1989. The film crew was unable to film the mirror because the fire extinguishing equipment sprayed them, for no reason except the possibility that Marilyn Monroe did not like the man in drag that portrayed her in the reenactment. This conclusion was provided by a psychic who sensed Marilyn's dislike for the cross-dresser. After several tries to film the mirror, they moved their operation one floor up to film a similar mirror.

The team of ghost hunters then proceeded to the ninth floor, where they investigated the legendary "haunted room." This was the room used by the actor Montgomery Clift during the filming of the movie classic, From Here to Eternity. Known as a serious actor, Clift learned to play a trumpet for his role in the movie. History tells of him practicing his lines for the film. Guests complained of his nocturnal trumpet practice sessions, but the hotel personnel were unable to curtail the actor.

Staff reported seeing his form in the hallway leading to his room, and others reported odd blasts from a trumpet late in the night. Could these be signs that his troubled spirit still wanders the old hotel?

In the room, the team conducted more experiments and a trumpet was brought in, in hopes that its presence might stimulate some type of psychic reaction. A seance was conducted by Debbie Senate in hopes of opening a channel of communication with whatever presence occupied the hotel. The room seemed to become strangely cold in the dim candle light. The team members held hands as Debbie slumped forward and then went into a deep trance. In several moments her face seemed to change A spirit did come forth but it seemed reluctant to say who it was or why it was here. It spoke of children that were not taken care of, fathered but not recognized. Then it was gone. Each of the team members felt a presence in the room. The next morning the trumpet was found on the carpet several feet from were it had been placed. It had been moved; whose hands touched it? Could it have been the hand of the late actor Montgomery Clift?

In evaluating the evidence collected in the 24-hour investigation it was determined that something does indeed haunt the Roosevelt Hotel.

Phantom Horseman of Griffith Park

A curse was launched in 1863 that has ensnared the owners of the 3,000-acre tract of land known today as Griffith Park. The awful hex was cast by a 17 year old blind girl, named Dona Petranilla Feliz, upon Don Antonio Colonel. Her father had died of smallpox that year, and he had deeded the estate to this friend Don Antonio. He had taken care of his relatives but, somehow he had overlooked poor Dona Petranilla. She cursed the land, saying that no good would ever come to those who owned the tract.

Though many believe the legendary curse to be only so much folklore, a number of strange disasters have come to those who have owned the estate. Many linked to the land met untimely ends due to accidents and the hand of man. Some say that Don Antonio haunts the land, riding his horse over its many trails. Leon Baldwin bought the rancho — bad luck swept over him, breaking his fortune before an outlaw gunned him down.

Next the land was purchased by Colonel Griffith J. Griffith. Right after buying the land the curse struck again in the form of a violent rain storm that caused wide spread destruction. Some say the ghost of Don Antonio directed the havoc. In 1896, Colonel Griffith gave the vast estate to the city of Los Angeles for use as a city park. This act didn't save him from the curse of Dona Petranilla. He served two years in prison for the attempted murder of his wife. His reputation was ruined from that day on. Horace Bell, a colorful pioneer newspaperman, wrote that the city council members who attended the fiesta that followed the donation of the land were followed by the mounted ghost of the enraged Don Antonio as they left the party!

From that time on people have reported seeing phantoms at Griffith Park; Sometimes a man on foot with a beard, other times the ghostly image of a woman in white, the wandering shade of Dona Petranilla. The most observed spectre is of a man riding the hills.

One eyewitness is Ms. Peggy Richards. An apartment manager who uses the Griffith trails, saw the ghost twice and believes it may be the spirit of Colonel Griffith himself. "I have been riding in Griffith Park since 1974. After working all day I would come home and take my horse out for a short ride to relax after work. I never felt frightened riding my horse Mia, she would always let me know if anyone or anything was hiding in the bushes way before we got close enough to be in danger. I have had streakers try to scare me but, Mia would always point her ears and snort before we got into their range. We would ride along the skyline trail that runs on top of the hills on the Glendale side of the park, looking down on Travel Town."

"One evening in the late fall, about dusk, I was riding east to go home on skyline trail when I saw this beautiful gaited black bay walking horse with a rider coming toward us. Mia was not afraid. I could see in the dim light of dusk that the bridle and saddle were of Spanish influence with a lot of silver too, with braided hair, leather reins and a long braided quirt (whip). There was a small silver bit."

"The rider had a silver Stetson (at least 25x), brown jacket, brown pants and brown cowboy boots. The horse was almost all black with light brown highlights on his muzzle and legs. I couldn't really see any feature on the rider's face. After we passed, I turned around and he had disappeared. My horse was not upset at this."

"Years later I was riding the trail that goes around the old abandoned zoo at dusk — it was about 7:30 in the summer. He rode right by me, the same horse and tack, and he was wearing the same clothes. I never took my eyes off of them, and they both, horse and rider, vanished right in front of my eyes as soon as they passed by me. There was a cold chill in the air as they passed. My horse never flinched. This time I noticed the saddle was a flat plantation saddle like the style used in the old South — it had no horn but it wasn't a true English Saddle."

"The ghost gave me the impression that he was having a good time. I could still not see his face very well." The

witness drew a picture of the image she encountered on the
skyline trail. From the type of horse, and the style of rig and
saddle, it seems to be a Yankee rather than a Spanish Don.
The ghost may not be the doomed Don Antonio but the
restless Colonel Griffith, still riding the estate he gave up so
long ago.

The ghost may well be some other hapless phantom who
enjoyed riding in life and continues his hobby in the afterlife.
The rig seems to indicate that it may well be someone from
our own century. Perhaps a businessman or silent movie star
who rides on the trails on set days and times. It is rather
common for a ghost to be mistaken for some famous person
linked to a site. I call this the 'George Washington effect'.
Washington may have spent one night in an old Inn and,
years later, they hear ghostly footsteps, So the owners of the
Inn jump to the conclusion that the pacing footsteps could
only be the worried footfalls of General Washington, pacing
the floor before a battle against the British. In fact the pacing
might be the unhappy ghost of some Ingaft Van Glaay, a
stable hand who hung himself over a lost love in 1802. But,
who would you like haunting your house? The first president
of the nation of some unknown Dutch teenager? I feel that
this might account for the many sightings of Washington,
Lincoln, and movie stars like Rudolph Valentino.

The Ghosts of Los Encinos

The young woman saw him standing near the gravel roadway, near the trunk of an ancient pepper tree. He was dressed as a monk with a cowl and robes. He wasn't looking at her, he was staring toward the highway. It was a cool, windy afternoon, but the woman noticed that none of the monk's clothing was affected by the wind. As she watched, the image started to walk and, as it did, it slowly became transparent and dissolved into the shadows of the trees. The apparition had been visible for only five or six seconds. It was only one of several reports of ghosts at the Los Encinos State Park in Encino, California. The park is gaining a reputation as one of the more haunted places in San Fernando Valley.

The five acre historic park was purchased by the State of California in 1949, and contains three historic buildings: the 1849 de la Osa Adobe, the limestone Gardiner house, and the 1797 one room stone hut built by Francisco Reyes. Each building has it's own distinctive legends and lore, and each, if the stories are to be believed, has it's own ghost.

The oldest structure has the most persistent haunt, that of a phantom blacksmith who still pounds upon his anvil from time to time. One woman visiting the site felt an icy cold wind as she approached the small building. She couldn't get close to it. "Something very terrible happened here," she said, her arms covered with goose bumps." I feel someone died here — it was very painful, and he begged for mercy!" Others pausing at he door have heard the whispered voices of people speaking in Spanish. Who they are and why they continue to haunt the building is unknown.

The long one-story adobe was built by Don Vicente de la Osa, and is made up of nine rooms. Even this adobe must have been cramped for Vincent and his wife Rita; they had fourteen children. A psychic visiting the old adobe house felt an icy presence in the bedroom. "It was a woman," she commented after the tour of the site. "She is very unhappy

about something to do with land and horses. I feel she died very young." She went on to describe a short, raven-haired woman. Though the ghost didn't seem to be attached to the de la Osa family, she may have well been a part of the staff of the Butterfield stagecoach station that was established at the adobe in 1858. Perhaps a traveler who missed the stage and continues to wander the adobe for a stagecoach that will never come.

The most recent sighting of phantoms centers on the French Provincial limestone house built in the 1870's by Eugene Gardiner. For years the house has been closed to the public, but in that time visitors have seen faces in the windows on the second floor of the structure. This was seen when the place was locked and secured. A visiting psychic saw three children at a window; two girls and a boy. "They are trapped here for some reason." The psychic said. "They are waiting for someone to come for them." She feels that some disaster or accident had taken them very quickly. Other visitors have seen faces at the window as well. With renovation, the Gardiner house is now open to the public, and it is possible that reports of hauntings will increase as tourists now can walk through the building.

The Flying Dutchman of the Mojave

In 1855 Secretary of War Jefferson Davis (later the first and last president of the ill fated Confederacy) proposed using camels to improve transportation in the Southwest and California. Congress appropriated $30,000 (then a great deal of money) to purchase and import camels and organize a camel corps to operate in the west. Two shipments of animals were brought from Egypt and landed in Texas. In 1857 Edward Fitzgerald Beale brought twenty- eight camels to California overland from San Antonio, Texas. The new camel unit was stationed at Fort Tejon, near Lebec on what is today Interstate Five. The camel corps were used to establish express route, carry supplies and convey surveying parties. Though the camels proved themselves ideal at crossing the dry trails of the Southwest, they were unpopular with the soldiers and civilians who favored mules and horses. In the dark days of the Civil War, the prejudice against the camels was so high that the remaining animals were driven to Benicia and sold at auction. Many were purchased by mining companies to carry supplies to remote camps in Nevada and the deserts of California.

Some of these camels are thought to have escaped. For years, camels were sighted in the Mojave; several were reported at the turn of the century. The last confirmed sighting took place in 1913. Camels seen today may be ghosts.

One legendary animal, with an odd white band, is linked to a terrible tragedy. The tale holds that in the 1850s an officer in the camel corps grew disgusted at the inability of new recruits to learn how to ride the beasts. Growing upset with one particularly dense enlisted man, the officer ordered that he ride the wildest camel in the herd. As the savage creature was roped and held down by a dozen men, the enlisted man was forced to mount the camel. The officer then ordered that the mans legs be lashed together, the rope passing under the camel's mid-section. The soldier would learn how to ride

camels or else! The camel was released and the brawling animal rocked to its feet and stood trembling for a long moment. Its maddened eyes flashed with hate, then he took off into the vastness of the desert. The other soldiers mounted mules, horses, and camels and rode in pursuit, as they jeered and laughed at the poor soldier's fright. As the day progressed, the laughter ceased as the terror-stricken animal outran them all. After several hours they lost complete track of the camel and his rider, still tied to the saddle. For three days and nights they searched and never found a trace of the pair. It was assumed then that the soldier must have died of thirst by then, and his bones were picked clean by scavengers. When the whitened skeleton fell away, all that was left were the leg and hip bones still lashed to the animal. The band of white reported around the camel could only be the remains of the ill-fated soldier.

This tragedy seems to have resulted in a ghost, the ghost of the camel and the bones of the rider. This phenomenon has been dubbed "The Flying Dutchman of the Desert."

Sightings of this take place every year, seen only on lonely highways in the Mojave Desert. Some report the racing camel traveling parallel to the road at speeds up to sixty miles per hour! Speeds impossible for a real camel. Perhaps the two-humped bactrian was not a regular camel at all but a camel from Hell.

The Ghost of the Leonis Adobe

The young couple visited the two story adobe on a rainy afternoon. To them it was a chance to get away from their responsibilities at the hospital; to relax and enjoy each other's company. The old adobe in Calabasas had intrigued them every time they had passed the place on their way home. Now they had the time to visit the restored historic home and discover its secrets. There were no other visitors on that day and only a single volunteer docent was there as they entered and signed in. The volunteer told them only the barest of facts about the 1844 adobe hacienda and it's builder, Don Miguel Leonis. They toured the museum without a guide. They were enjoying their time, slowly examining the rooms of the house museum. They made their way upstairs and viewed the rooms. They were drawn to a large bedroom where they noticed a large bearded man asleep in one of the beds. The figure was so still that at first they thought it was a dummy. But, it was so lifelike that it captured the couple's interest. They saw that the image wasn't a dummy, it was slowly breathing. They smiled and whispered that it must be an old caretaker who had gone to sleep on a lazy rainy afternoon. Then they saw the man gasp and begin to shake with a sudden seizure. The young couple had seen this before. A barricade stood at the entrance of the room. The man ran down the stairs, taking them two at a time. "There's a man up here in trouble!" He yelled at the top of his lungs. "Unlock the barricade!" The volunteer was taken aback, and she grabbed her keys and followed the couple back up the stairs. "Who is it?" the volunteer asked. "Why, your care-taker or your handyman I guess," the man answered. "He's sleeping in the large bedroom upstairs."

They ran to the room only to find that there was no one there. There were no men on the site that day, and the couple were the first visitors of the day. The staircase is the only one leading to the second story. All three had seen no one else in the building. They checked the room and found that the bed

had not been disturbed. The figure had vanished! Who could it have been? Is it possible that it was the restless spirit of Don Miguel Leonis? The couple didn't know that he died in that room, in great agony, from injuries suffered in a mysterious accident.

Some believe that Miguel Leonis was murdered in 1889. He had many enemies, due to the dictatorial way he controlled the vast El Escorpion Rancho. He was called "The King of Calabasas," and ruled over his lands with a mercenary retinue of Mexican gunfighters. He was a Basque immigrant who never learned to speak Spanish or English well. He married an Indian widow, Espiritu Chijulla, and through this marriage he came to own 1100 acres of land and livestock. With this as a base he quickly grew to be one of the richest men in Los Angeles County. But, his many lawsuits and battles with settlers took their toll on him.

His wagon overturned on the Cahuenga Pass, crushing him. Some believe it was not an accident, but someone spooking the team of horses causing the mishap. He lived three pain-filled days before he died in the room in which the couple had experienced seeing the image. His Indian wife held onto the ranch until her death in 1906.

It was after her death that the first reports of ghosts began to circulate, and these encounters continue to the present day. The first stories told of footsteps pacing the second floor at all hours, and of doors slamming shut by themselves on windless days. Both visitors and volunteers at the Leonis adobe have seen dark figures that vanish away as well as hearing sobbing when there is no one around. Some of the accounts are as chilling as any found in haunted houses of fiction. Several years ago a five year old girl visiting the house started to scream and point at the bed in the master bedroom. She said that there was a man on the bed. A man with a black beard and covered with bloody bandages. She described the death scene that occurred a century before. Some have told of seeing the image of a woman in a long black dress standing on the balcony. For most of her adult life Espiritu Leonis wore nothing but black. Volunteers at the historic residence agree that something walks the halls at the adobe. One account even states that it may have a helpful nature. In the 1960's, when the house was being restored, one of the caretakers was standing on the balcony when she felt two powerful hands on her shoulders pulling her away from the wooden balcony rails. They discovered the next day that the railing had rotted through and, if the woman had leaned on the rail, it may well have broken. The ghost may have saved her life!

The Leonis Adobe is open to the public every Wednesday through Sunday, from 1:00 to 4:00 p.m., at 23537 Calabasas Road in Calabasas. Tour the remarkable adobe and home, and be on the lookout for a strange sound, a column of cold air and the figure of the bearded man. Ask the volunteers about the legends of the ghosts. Some are ready to talk about all the odd things that have been reported over the years. Others are reluctant to speak of the phantom believing it might reflect badly on the historic homesite. One thing everyone can agree upon is that the Leonis Adobe is a very special place.

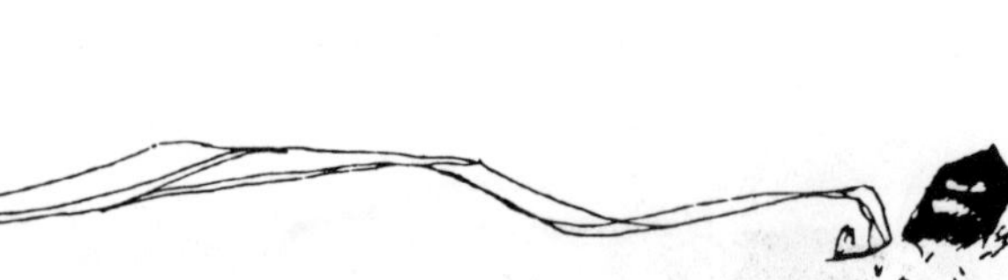

In Search of Kabar's Ghost

They held hands tightly in the cool, fog shrouded after-noon. The air took on a biting chill as the medium hung her head low and swayed back and forth in deep meditation. "He's here," she murmured over the steady rustle of leaves of the surrounding trees. "I can feel his presence," added another. Then a startling shriek filled the air. "He's licking my ankles!" cried one of the group, "Oh my God, he's licking both my ankles." There was nothing there to see, but she swears she could feel a moist tongue gently lapping at her feet. Had the group succeeded in contacting the restless spirit of Kabar, the dog once owned by silent star Rudolph Valentino?

The group had met at the Los Angeles Pet Memorial Park at Calabasas to hold a seance for a dog! Here, on Old Scandia Lane, the SPCA maintains a large pet cemetery, where over 27,000 pets have been interred for over seventy years. Many famous animals have found their final resting place here. They range from Jay "Tonto" Silverheel's horse "Scout" to "Blinky" the friendly hen. The pets of such stars as Gloria Swanson, Eva Gabor and Bob Newhart are buried at the Memorial Park.

Of all the animals resting at the cemetery, none have been encountered as ghosts as often as Kabar, Valentino's faithful Doberman. Legend holds that on the night of August 23, 1926, Kabar let out with a terrible howl, so loud that actress Beatrice Lillie, driving her car past the Valentino estate was so frightened she almost ran off the mountain road. At the same moment, in a New York hospital 3,000 miles away, the silent movie "heart-throb" had passed away of pleurisy.

Dogs are very psychic animals. The history of psychic phenomena is filled with examples of dogs knowing when their masters have 'passed over,' In 1923, Lord Carnarvon, who funded the expedition to find the tomb of Egyptian Pharaoh Tutankhamen, entered the tomb. He was one of the first to set foot in the tomb. Some said that the royal burial chamber was protected by a terrible curse. In two months the fifty-six year old Lord was dead of a simple insect bite! At the exact moment Carnarvon died in Cairo, his dog in England let out a terrible howl and dropped dead on the rug before the fireplace! Dogs are special animals, and over the many thousands of years they have associated with man a special link has been forged.

Kabar lived another three years, becoming part of the legal estate of Valentino. On February 2nd, 1929, he passed on to finally join his beloved master in death. His funeral was one of the most lavish in the history of the pet cemetery. His headstone bears the simple epitaph: "Kabar, Rudolph Valentino's Dog."

After the sudden and unexpected death of the silent screen star, numerous psychics and spiritualists claimed that they were in communication with Valentino. One even produced a book he swore had been dictated to him by the movie idol from beyond the grave. Character actor Harry Carry once rented the Valentino Mansion. He reported seeing the image of the silent lover dressed in the costume of a gaucho. The ghost was seen by Carry's young son as well. Valentino's phantom is perhaps the most seen ghost in the history of Hollywood, having been spotted at hotels, restaurants and film studios throughout the film capital. After 1929, many of these seances also produced apparitions of the ghost dog Kabar.

On May 6, 1948, a group of spiritualists gathered at Valentino's mansion to celebrate what would have been his fifty-third birthday. During the affair, in which skeptical members of the press were present, several mediums told of seeing the ghost of Valentino. None could agree on what he was wearing. Finally someone shouted out, "I see Rudy's dog! It's a noble beast." Another announced that "Kabar is licking my face!" Several witnesses swore they saw the image of a large dog leap through a closed window. Many of the newsmen were skeptical that Rudy or Kabar had attended the seance; they had seen nothing. But, towards the end of the night, one photographer took an infrared picture of the medium, Carol McKinstry, in front of a huge portrait of Valentino. The photographer, a well-known professional, was amazed when he developed the film and saw a glowing ball of light in the painting over the picture's heart. He was at a loss to explain the odd glow.

Mr. Carl M. who lives in Encino, has visited the pet cemetery many times over the years. His beloved collie is buried there. On three separate occasions he claimed that a large Doberman has run toward him from the area where Kabar is interred. The friendly-looking animal seems to be looking for someone, then vanishes. "The first time I saw it, I thought it was a stray just running around," he recalls. "It just ran up behind the trees and disappeared."

Hearing the stories of the large dog phantom in the memorial park, a group of spiritualists gathered to try to rescue the wandering spirit of the dog and reunite him with his famous master. After finding the grave, the group formed a circle and attempted to communicate with the celebrity hound. After several felt what they believe was the tongue of Kabar, the medium spoke to the ghostly animal and directed it on towards the light of heaven, where he could at last find the master he sought. Did they really raise the spirit of Kabar? Who can say? But, since the seance, the misty figure of a Doberman has not been seen.

San Fernando Mission

The woman felt eyes watching her as she cleaned the room. There was no one there but the feeling persisted that she was not alone. Turning, she saw the shadow of a tall man on the wall. The figure slowly vanished away into nothingness. This was one of several ghosts seen and felt at the historic Mission of San Fernando in Mission Hills.

Established on September 8, 1797, by Fray Fermin Lasuen, it was one of four established that year by the energetic successor to Fray Junipero Serra. Like many of the California Missions, there was a period of spectacular growth followed by a long, painful decline, ending in abandonment and decay. The buildings were the abode of owls and bats in those times and there are frequently told stories of lost gold and wandering ghosts who were attached to the place.

Ghosts are found at many of the missions — San Fernando is no exception. One story focuses on the long building with its long row of arches. It is the tale of the Cat Woman.

Long ago (no one is sure of the date), an elderly woman took care of the stray cats that gathered at the old mission. She would sweep the archway and left food for the animals. The cats always gathered around whenever they saw the lady approach. She kept the place clean, so the mission fathers did not hamper her activities. As happens to all, one day she didn't come to feed her cats. She had passed over into the land of shadows. But people still see the woman, still shuffling along, still doing her duty to her small charges. Now, as in life, she is still surrounded by phantom cats! The cats, out of devotion, have followed her on into death! One young woman, driving down San Fernando Blvd. late one night, saw the image near the archway. As she passed, she said that the eyes of the cats (there must have been twenty of them) "glowing red like hot coals!"

Another local resident recalls being chased through the park near the Mission by the black-clad woman and her wild

army of felines! "My dog just took off running the other way!" he recalls after a quarter of a century. "I saw her and I swear she had no face!" The phantom, called by locals the 'Cat Woman', has been seen off and on for decades.

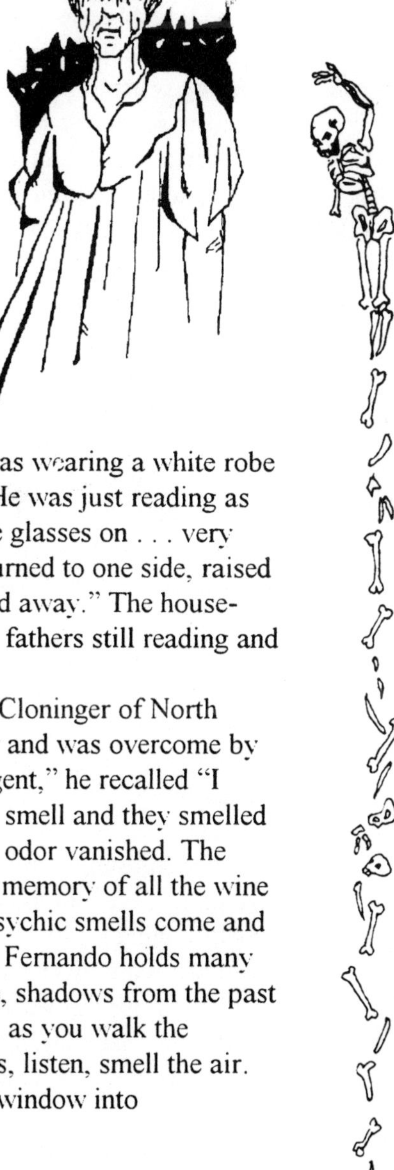

Psychics visiting the old mission have encountered a ghostly monk in the long convento building - several times in the library. These well-read ghosts seem attached to their books. "I walked into the room, the one with all the books . . . and I saw him standing in one corner of the room with a book. He was wearing a white robe and he seemed to be sixty years old. He was just reading as he stood there. He had these cute little glasses on . . . very small glasses. As I watched, he just turned to one side, raised his head up to look at me and vanished away." The house-wife believes she saw one of the early fathers still reading and studying the books he loved in life.

One psychic researcher, Mr. Brian Cloninger of North Hollywood, visited the old wine cellar and was overcome by the odor of wine. "It was strong, pungent," he recalled "I asked several of the visitors about the smell and they smelled it too." After a time the overpowering odor vanished. The smell may well have been the psychic memory of all the wine production of the mission long ago. Psychic smells come and go in a split second. The Mission San Fernando holds many mysteries and, if the accounts are true, shadows from the past linger there. Visit the old mission and, as you walk the grounds, for a moment close your eyes, listen, smell the air. Perhaps this special place is indeed a window into California's past.

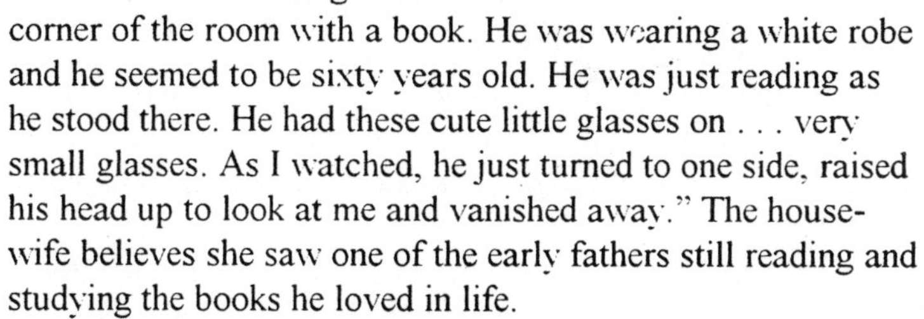

The Ghost of William S. Hart

The white house gleamed in the blistering heat of a noon-day sun. The house seemed to resemble a European castle looming over the park. The home was built 70 years ago by a silent movie star in rural Newhall, California. His name was William S. Hart, and it was his wish that his house be open to the public as a museum. He died in 1946, and some believe his spirit continues to wander the home he loved.

Many film historians credit the creation of the western film to William S. Hart. He was raised in the West, and insisted that his films depict the gritty West he knew as a child. His films had a raw violent edge, in some ways resembling the films of Clint Eastwood. Hart's classic role was that of 'Two Gun Bill,' a good man forced into a life of crime, who redeems himself through the love of a woman.

He began to make films as early as 1914 and continued until 1926. In the 20's Hart was one of the richest stars in Hollywood, ranking with such movie greats as Chaplin and Pickford.

Never comfortable in Hollywood, he purchased a ranch in Newhall to escape from the fast life that was slowly encroaching upon the movie colony.

On his ranch he even filmed several of his later films, including the classic western 'Tumble Weeds,' his last motion picture.

For years rumors of ghosts have been linked to the Hart Ranch and the hilltop house. There were stories of odd smells, such as coffee in the kitchen, where coffee had not been brewed in over forty years. There were sightings of a ghostly figure identified as that of William S. Hart himself. Some said that a strange "feeling" was encountered in the bedrooms and a psychic even claimed to have felt a phantom dog.

An officer assigned to guard the many treasures in the Hart Mansion was walking though the house when he saw a figure drifting though the bedroom used by Hart's sister Mary. It so

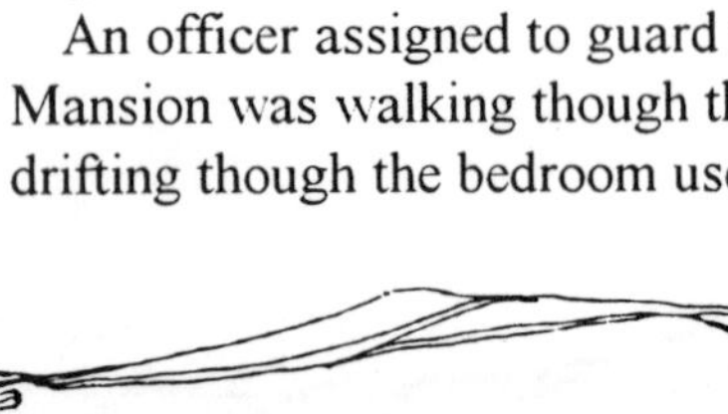

spooked him that he asked to be reassigned to another duty rather than chance another meeting with the spectre. One of the visitors touring the house glanced into the very same room and saw a misty, cloud-like form hovering over the bed . In a second it was gone! Though the docent guides do not include the ghost stories in their tour, they will tell the accounts if asked. They tell of how the candles have moved seemingly by themselves, on the breakfast table. One little girl visiting the estate was relaxing by the building called the bunk house, where Hart held parties at times. She pointed into nothing and asked about the "big doggies." She didn't know that the path next to the 'bunk house' was used every day by William S. Hart's two great dane dogs.

In a tour of the site, a psychic researcher was surprised to see a shadowy form walk along a balcony toward the projection room where Hart had entertained guests by showing them some of his films. The figure wasn't dressed as 'Two Gun Bill.' He wore a sweater and a pair of tan pants. The form vanished into the door of the small room without opening it. This took place during a tour of the site with a room full of people, yet no one else saw or reported the ghostly sighting. Still, it happened when the guide was talking and showing some of the many interesting photographs on the walls. The witness was the only one looking up at the balcony above. The phantom was visible for about three seconds and wasn't that distinct. Could it have been the ghost of William S. Hart, perhaps? It would not be the only sighting to have been reported. A volunteer at the house, Mrs. Dorris Reynolds, claimed to have been resting in the large parlor when she looked up to see the image, clear in the daylight, of William S. Hart reading the newspaper. She watched for well over a minute. The image never looked at Mrs. Reynolds. After a time the figure vanished away.

Others have noticed objects move about but nothing as dramatic as the image of Hart reading his newspaper or rushing to his projection room. If he does haunt, he is certainly a ghost comfortable in the house he loved for so long.

Simi Valley Phone Call From the Dead

In all the years I have spent investigating the unknown, the strangest story I have ever heard was that of a phone call seemingly from beyond death! Several books have been written that touch upon the subject but this was the first time I had contact with someone on the receiving end of what can only be called 'long, long distance.

The call in question was received by the then manager of a Simi Valley health spa in 1979. The call came on a Monday morning just as Ms. Linda L. was coming through the door to open the spa for the day. It was ringing when she unlocked the door, and continued to ring (this was before answering machines were commonplace). At last, with the alarms disarmed and the lights on, the manager could pick up the receiver. The voice on the phone was weak and thin. Linda believed it was that of an elderly woman. "Can you help me?" the voice asked "Can you help me?" it said. The manager was sure she repeated the sentence twice. The voice went on to say that she was ill and that she needed to get in better shape. She said that she was having trouble with her heart and kidneys and that her doctor urged her to get into a program of exercise.

As manager of the spa Linda, had received many calls from older residents and the spa had developed several plans for senior citizens. As a matter of policy Linda asked for the woman's name. In a weak voice, the manager thought she said "Mary." When she ask if it was "Mary," the woman on the telephone corrected her. The name was "Merle." She even spelled it out. The last name was a common one with a common spelling. Next, Linda asked her for her phone number. At first the elderly woman was reluctant to give the number but in the end she gave a local number. "Merle" promised to come in the next day at a given time to work out her needs. Two days passed and elderly woman failed to keep her appointment at the spa. The spa always calls back potential members in hopes of answering any questions and maybe re-stimulating interest in membership. Linda called the number Wednesday afternoon and a man answered. From the tone of his voice the manager believed that he too was elderly. She asked if she could speak to his wife. He told her that his wife had passed away fifteen years ago. Linda then asked if someone named Merle lived at the address, thinking that the woman might be a sister or other relative living in the home. At this point the man began to cry. He said that his wife was named Merle, and that she had passed away of a sudden heart attack. Shaken by this, the manager asked if she had perhaps gotten a wrong number and had fallen into a bizarre coincidence of names.

The man confirmed the number and demanded to know how she had gotten it as it was an unlisted number. She tried to tell him but he hung up. Linda reached for the telephone directory and found that the number was indeed unlisted. Was it an elaborate hoax or did the spa manager really receive a phone call from the Great Beyond? She can still recall the frail voice of the woman and the tears in the man's voice. She believes it was a ghost, unable to accept her death, still trying to secure help so she can "get back in shape." Ghostly accounts like this have been recorded for many years by psychic researchers from all over the world. It seems that under the right conditions, those who have crossed over into that other land can, telephone the world of the living for brief conversations. Still, what seemed believable happening in London, England, seems strange and out of place in suburban Simi Valley. Of all the tales I have heard, this one causes me to speculate most on what awaits us all down the road we must all one day tread.

The Ghost of Jesse James Stalks Somis

I watched, fascinated, as the planchet of the Ouija Board slowly moved over the letters spelling out: T-O-N-I-G-H-T J-E-S-S-E W-I-L-L B-E B-A-D. As the marker reached the last letter of the message Rod screamed out with blood flowing from his lip. "I'm bleedin" he cried out. Could it be that this young man was the victim of the long dead outlaw Jesse James?

It began simply enough with a phone call in the middle of the night. A family in Somis had been "playing" with a Ouija Board and began to receive messages from someone, or something, that claimed to be the shade of the bandit Jesse James.

One of the group working the Ouija Board at the time was a young police officer named 'Rod.' As a member of the law enforcement community he first scoffed at the odd messages, but in time his skepticism turned to fear and then lastly terror. Once the force calling itself 'Jesse' learned that Rod was a 'lawman,' it focused all of its hate against him. Objects were seen moving, and once the young man was struck so hard that he was pushed several feet into a tree trunk. "There was nothin' there — yet it struck me so hard it lifted off the ground." During one argument with the ghost, Rod felt a sudden pain in his back. It burned and caused him to raise his shirt. A round welt about the size of a nickel marred his back. The Ouija Board spelled out an odd message: W-H-Y A-I-N-T Y-O-U D-E-A-D?

Seemingly the ghost had used a phantom revolver to attempt bushwhacking the young man from behind! With phenomena reported by a trained observer such as a police officer, I felt that this case should be investigated as soon as possible. I arranged for a meeting at the Somis home where the strange events took place. I can still remember the long cold drive to Somis in the light rain. With me was my wife, Debbie Christenson Senate; her psychic gifts might help to sort out the mysterious events that enveloped the ranch. I

began to wonder why I had committed myself to this investigation.

Stories of Ouija Board messages are almost always simple subconscious messages with little basis in fact. Still, the case with its link to physical phenomena was very different from other cases I had investigated in the past. If it was really the ghost of Jesse James, I had resolved to prove or disprove its existence, even if it meant putting myself at physical risk!

We found the ranch house as the rain began to fall hard and fast. Debbie and I made our way to the porch, the door opened to a comfortable living room set with a western decor. The family and friends waited to give us their account of the events they had witnessed before attempting to once again contact the shade of 'Jesse James.' We met Rod, the young policeman. He told us nervously, "If you would have asked me about this three months ago, I would have said it's all bull — but not now. If this ever gets out, I would have a lot of problems on the force. They would force me to go in for psychological testing and all kinds of stuff. I could lose my job, but I saw it and felt it. I'm the world's biggest skeptic until I was hit by this thing. I saw things happen with my own eyes. So, whatever you do, don't use my real name." I promised him complete anonymity —giving him the name 'Rod' in this published account.

We gathered in the living room to once again attempt to make contact with the outlaw's spirit. In preparation for this challenge I developed a list of twenty questions that I believe only the real Jesse James or a trained historian could answer. This involved a week of research on the outlaw and his times. Knowing that the real Jesse James was a passionate Southerner, I couched the questions in such a way that it would infuriate anyone from his home state of Missouri. The group placed their hands on the pointer, and slowly the device began to trace out the letters to the name 'Jesse.' I asked if I could ask him some questions about his life. The pointer moved to "Yes."

1. "What was Jesse's middle name?" Ouija Board: "Edie." Real answer: Woodson.

2. "What was Jesse's father's occupation?" Ouija board: "Minister." Real answer: Minister.

3. "What was the Name of Jesse's mother?" Ouija Board: "No" response. Real answer: Zerelda.

4. "What was the Name of Jesse's wife?" Ouija Board: "Zee." Real answer: Zee.

5. "What type pistol did Jesse carry?" Ouija Board: "Fayeone." Real answer: Smith & Wesson 45

6. "What type of pistol did Frank James carry?" Ouija Board: "Pynmayno." Real Answer: Remington 44.

7. "Who was Bill Anderson?" Ouija Board: "A good friend." Real answer: Confederate guerilla leader in Missouri during the Civil War.

8. "What did Bill Anderson have tied to his horse's bridle?" Ouija Board: No response. Real answer: Scalps of Yankees.

9. " Who was Jesse's commanding officer?" Ouija Board: No response. Real answer: William Quantrill.

10. " What was 'Order No. 11?" Ouija Board: No response. Real answer: The hated Yankee order evicting all Missourians who favored the South in the Civil War. Many farms were burned and people's lives ruined — the memory of this still angers people in Missouri today.

11. "What happened when Jesse tried to surrender to the Yankees at the end of the War Between the States?" Ouija Board: "Shot." Real answer: Shot in the chest while carrying a white flag.

12. "What was the name of Jesse's favorite horse?" Ouija Board: "Henry." Real answer: Steve:

13. "What town did Jesse visit in California?" Ouija Board: "Santa Paula." Real answer: Paso Robles.

14. "U.S. Agents tossed a bomb into Jesse's house in 1875. Where was his mother injured?" Ouija Board: "Eye." Real answer: Right arm blown off.

15. " What were the names of Jesse's children?" Ouija Board: "Jesse and Anne." Real answer: Jesse and Mary.

16. "Where were they born?" Ouija Board: no response. Real answer: Nashville.

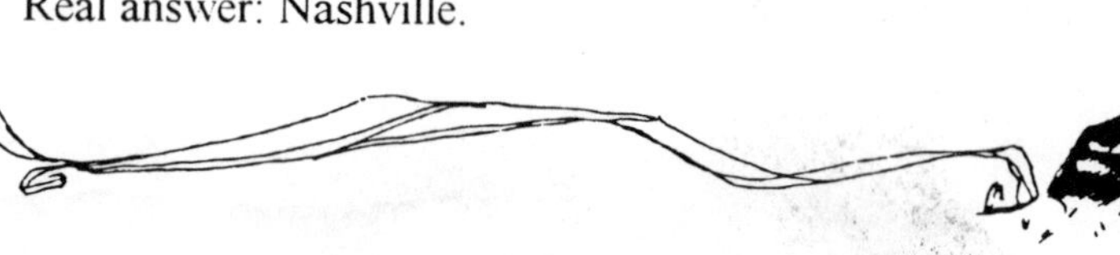

17. "Name the Younger Brothers" (part of Jesse's gang). Ouija board: "Jim, Cole, Bob." Real answer: Jim, Cole and Bob Younger.

18." Who was General Thomas Ewing?" Ouija Board: "A bad man." Real answer: Yankee General who issued General Order No. 11.

19. "Who was Frank James' favorite author?" Ouija Board: No response. Real answer: Shakespeare.

20. "Who was John Trammell?" Ouija Board: "A friend." Real answer: Jesse's black cook.

I attempted to anger the spirit by calling him 'a rebel and traitor to the Union.' His tone became hot. The words came fast and heated. To further infuriate the suspected spirit I called him and his bandit gang nothing but 'Southern Trash' hiding behind the flag of Dixie. The board spelled out the message that he would be 'bad' now as I challenged him to try to hurt me. The force calling itself Jesse turned its attack not on me but on Rod! Something seemed to hit him and once again he started to bleed from the lips. We ended the session at once.

Since then The group stopped the sessions and the spirit of Jesse James has not been summoned. Was the spirit of the western outlaw present in Somis? Who knows? The answers seem to reflect some of the basic history of the outlaw. I noticed a copy of the Time/Life book "The Outlaws" on a shelf in the living room. The facts in this book were found in the Ouija responses. The questions unanswered in the session were unavailable in this book. I feel that something very powerful was somehow released by the Ouija Board. Perhaps it still wanders the roadways of the small community, still armed with his phantom pistol, willing to "shoot it out" with any one who would dare mock him or his bandit ways. I can still feel the tense atmosphere in the living room, and the look of utter bewilderment on Rod's face. Debbie and I believe something was indeed present that night.

What really took place on the ranch in Somis? Was it really the spirit of Jesse James? I do not think so. The spirit seemed unable to answer basic questions about the life of the famed outlaw. As was pointed out by Mr. David Roell of the Astrology Center of Southern California, " a Jesse James who doesn't know his mother's name is not Jesse James." As Mr. Roell pointed out, why would the shade of Jesse James wish to haunt an obscure town he knew nothing about in California? Several different theories might explain the event. "Jesse" might be the spirit of an earthbound soul who has taken the identity of the outlaw for some reason, perhaps to be noticed. "Jesse" Might be some "elemental" spirit that was attracted to the Ouija board and decided to "play along for a while and cause some mischief. "Jesse" could be the spirit of a modern bandit, perhaps one killed in a confrontation with law enforcement officers. Maybe this spirit admired the western badman in life and took his name in death. "Jesse" might also be a thought form manifest by the collective sub-conscience of the people on the Ouija board. Perhaps the evil side of "Jesse" sprang from the deep sub-conscience of "Rod." For all we know, the thing calling itself "Jesse" may have been a demon right out of the fires of Hell. Those who are motivated to use a 'Ouija Board' should be very wary of what things come forth on such a device. Some believe that only 'Low Spirits' are attracted to such things, but I have witnessed some unique things come through the board at times. A few rules of thumb should be observed.

1) Never use a Ouija Board alone.

2) A third person, one not touching the pointer, should ask the questions and record the answers.

3) If anything 'Evil' or negative starts to come through the board, stop at once!

Some say that it is the Devil's own tool, but too many verses of poetry and sound advice have been recorded to dismiss them all together. Still, the unnerving fact remains that the Ouija Boards are manufactured in Salem, Massachusetts.

Port Hueneme's Haunted Mansion

The Port Hueneme Naval Construction Battalion base has a ghost performing maneuvers in the Officer's Club. Senator Thomas R. Bard's lavish three storied mansion was built in 1912. Some of the old-timers believe the noises and strange happening are caused by the old senator, distressed by the fact that his fine home was taken from the family by the Navy in World War II.

One bartender witnessed a light go on and off mysteriously. In May of 1978, the management clerk locked up the Bard Mansion late at night. Just as he was about to unlock his car in the parking lot, he glanced up at the building to see a light on in one of the third floor rooms. He knew he hadn't turned on the light and he was the only one with a key to that room. It was late, so he chose to go home rather than unlock the building, turn off the alarms, walk up to the third floor just to turn off one stray light. He would turn it off in the morning. The next day he was the first in the building and his first task he set for himself was to turn off the light in the attic. He climbed the stairs, unlocked the door and, when he got to the room, the light was off! That evening, after a long day he once again locked up and, once again in the parking lot he looked at the mansion and, once again the light was on. Now he was ready to confront the mystery first hand. He unlocked the house, made his way to the third floor—the light was burning and he had to use the light switch to turn it off. He glanced behind him and there was no one there.

One story tells of a customer who came out of the rest room and his face was as white as a sheet. He said that he had seen the ghost of a man in the mirror as he washed his hands.

Others recount hearing terrible screams coming from the kitchen. The odd sounds heard in the kitchen may well be the phantom sounds of the Chinese cook 'Ah Kim Chang'.

A group of ghost hunters received permission to spend the night of May 10, 1980, in the Bard Mansion. During the long night, they toured the building several times from basement to attic. Most of the team came to the conclusion that the third floor was the center of the haunting. One of the group saw an apparition of a woman slowly drift out of the 'School Room' on the third floor. Several members felt something cold on the stairway going up to the third floor. In the middle of the night a 'seance ' was held in the red room. The spirit of a Chinese servant named 'Ah Kim Chang' was manifest.

In 1977, a trio of investigators spent the night in the mansion, attempting to prove or disprove the existence of ghosts in the place. One of the team members, Laura Beagle, using infrared red film, caught a weird glowing illumination hovering in one of the hallways. She was at a loss to explain how the light appeared in the picture.

Who haunts the mansion? Some say it is the Senator himself angry that the US Navy now owns the lavish house he built. Others say it might be his son Robert who died young. Still other contend that it might be the restless ghost of the Chinese servant 'Chang' .

Many believe that it may well be the ghost of Elizabeth Bard, the senators wife, (who was called Molly) She was a staunch prohibitionist, against alcohol in any form. The strongest thing served at the mansion was lemonade. Perhaps her spirit is angered by the presence of "demon rum."

The Dark Lady of Ventura's Olivas Adobe

The adobe hacienda of Don Raymundo Olivas is furnished with antiques and displays of the last century, but if the stories are true, the historic museum is not empty of residents.

Some believe the ghostly resident is the spirit of Dona Teodora Olivas, the wife of the builder, Don Raymundo. One morning a witness in the courtyard was stunned to see the figure of a short woman, dressed in a white blouse and long grey skirt, walking into the kitchen. Even with doorways fitted with wrought iron fences to protect irreplaceable furnishings, the woman walked right through the iron fence into the kitchen.

Over the years numerous people have reported seeing a female image at the Olivas Adobe.

At 4:30 on December 10, 1989, an employee at the Olivas Adobe saw a female figure, who seemed to be in mourning clothes, glide into the master bedroom on the second floor. "I was on the balcony and, if this had been a mortal person, the weight of her footfalls surely would have drawn my attention."

"If it weren't for the lack of sound, and not being able to find the mysterious woman when I past the room she entered, as well as her attire, I might say she was mortal. She seemed very real and solid."

On December 10, 1989, a two-year-old said she saw someone in the upper window. Sarah came running toward the house and asked her mother, "Who is that?" as she pointed to an upstairs window. Her mother looked up at the children's room window and did not see anything. Sarah described the person, "She was nice and had nice clothes. She had a nice dress and nice hair."

Later a second witness of this same ghost contacted the adobe staff. She is Mrs. Shelly Navarro, a former employee of the park service. "There was always a feeling of being watched out here. The last day I was here, on a Friday, I

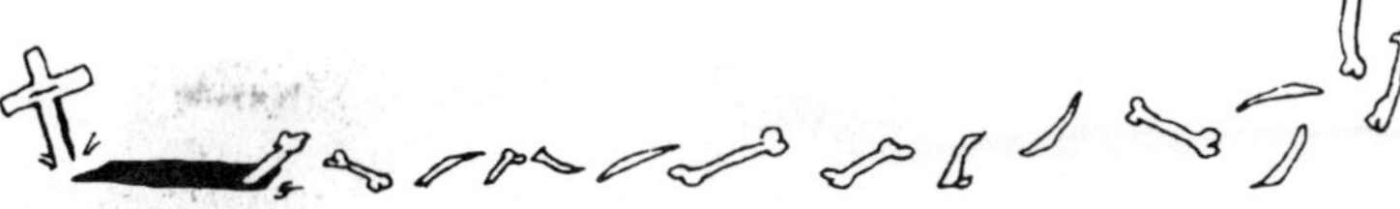

looked up toward the front of the house . . . at the last window I thought I saw a woman. Old, very old woman, gray tint to her. Black dress with white lace. I looked away then back and she was gone. It was only for a second, I got scared, I got chills down my spine." Hers would not be the last sighting.

Mrs. Dorris Reynolds, historic interpreter at the Olivas Adobe, arrived early to open up the historical residence. As she was unlocking the doors, she knew that she was the only person there. While attending to the downstairs section, she heard footsteps above her on the balcony. "A tourist must have gotten past me when my back was turned," she thought to herself. "I should let them know we are not yet open."

She went up the stairway to greet the early visitor as well as open the doors. As she was prepared to see someone, it came as shock to find no one there. There is only one stairway leading to the second story.

On May 23, 1987, Annette Morris toured the Olivas Adobe. During the two and a half hours she was there, she felt the following:

"It would appear from the atmosphere that a woman had a strong influence in the life of the house. The bedroom gives a feeling of sadness, yet love. Perhaps a woman lingering in illness, reluctant to leave her family to care for others.

The kitchen reflects somberness, a feeling of the spirit caring about the welfare of the family left behind. She makes her presence felt, if not seen, in the kitchen and dining areas.

She is a tall woman. She recovered from a serious illness. A very pleasant woman who had been very beautiful in youth. The ghost appeared in the upstairs bedroom for a brief second just to watch and make sure nothing was disturbed, then faded away. She is rooted to her family."

Mr. Ken Christenson had volunteered to help the Olivas Adobe docents put on one of the colorful evening programs one summer. Once the chairs and decorations were taken down and put away, he was in one of the last cars to pull out of the dark parking lot that night. When he looked back at the adobe, he saw a strange orange light come on in one of the

first floor room! Ken had a flashlight with him and pointed it towards the window and flashed twice. The light in the window went on and off twice as if to answer him. Others in the car saw the strange light as well.

Santa Paula's Glen Tavern Inn

Perhaps the most haunted structure in Ventura County is Santa Paula's Glen Tavern Inn. The tudor-style hotel was built in 1911, and almost from it's beginning, rumors of ghosts have swirled around the place. The former manager, Mrs. Dolores Diehl, confirmed that a number of guests have reported odd manifestations in their rooms late at night, and at least 75% of the hotel staff has encountered one of several phantoms that wander the inn.

Many of the reports center on room 307, where she claimed to have spoken to the phantom presence and learned that his name is "Calvin." She described the apparition as middle aged, with long hair and a pointed beard. One theory surrounding "Calvin" is that he was murdered in that room after an illegal poker game in which he may or may not have been cheating. Another theory holds that "Calvin" may have been part of the motion picture industry. In the early 1920s, dozens of western films were made in and around Santa Paula. Perhaps the persistent phantom was a member of the cast or crew of one of those films. The Glen Tavern Inn was the most elegant establishment in the era, and played host to many movie stars and companies.

In 1986, a group of students, investigating the reports of ghosts visited the inn. One student, using infrared film, photographed all of the rooms and places where ghosts have been sighted. When the film was developed, a strange image appeared in the photograph taken in room 307. The faint apparition seemed to be a man with long hair and a beard! Yet, when the student took the picture, she had been alone in the room.

Although most of the ghost sightings have revolved around room 307, other ghosts have been encountered throughout the historic inn. Visitors have witnessed a spoon fly across the dining area by itself! One waitress reported seeing chairs move by themselves in the restaurant late at night.

Skeptics derided the accounts, saying they were the

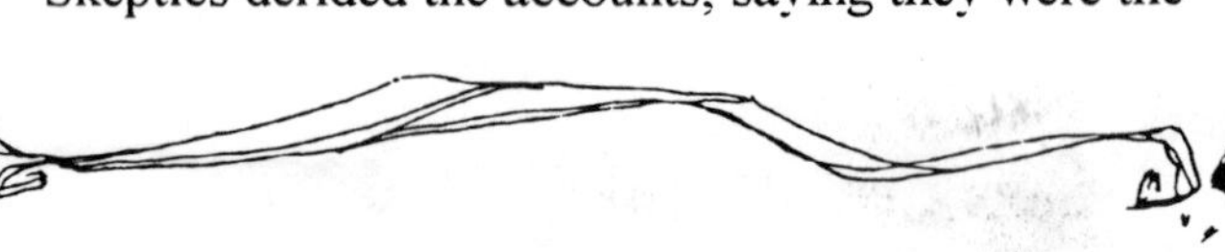

creation of the former management in an attempt to secure publicity and attract visitors. Though some of the reported ghosts may well have been glamorized, the vast majority seem to be real events witnessed by ordinary people. Hallucination and overactive imagination could account for some of these sightings, but not all. Debbie Christenson Senate spent several nights in the lobby of the old hotel. Once, at three a.m. she heard footsteps running down the stairs. She looked up, thinking it was one of the guests coming down for something. She heard the footfalls grow louder but she saw nothing there. The sounds went right by her but there was no one there! She paused, and said to herself, "I must be imagining things," then, the sounds came again! Now they were going up the stairs. As the invisible thing passed her on the foot of the stairs she felt a distinct chill sweep up the stairs. Checking with the hotel staff, she learned that this wasn't the first time the footsteps were encountered late at night.

By far, the most impressive sightings were those personally witnessed during the one year investigation of the Glen Tavern Inn.

Rumor holds that room 308 of the was used by the late magician Harry Houdini. The story is that Houdini was forced to spend the night at the place in the mid 1920's when the railroad line north was damaged in a rain storm. At that time the third floor was mostly attic space. Houdini wanted a place to store his magic props where he could watch over them so no one would discover his secrets.

I was never able to confirm that the great magician ever stopped in Santa Paula — but, the legend continued that he once slept in room 308 at some point in the inn's past.

On the nights of November 8th and 9th, 1987, my wife and I spent the weekend in the "Houdini Room" of the old inn. Debbie and I didn't want to sleep in the room. She claimed the room gave her the "creeps." That morning a strange thing did happen that I am at a loss to explain even after all these years. At about 8:40 AM, the bathroom door moved back and forth several times. At first I thought it was caused by me walking around in the bathroom after taking a shower. Debbie pointed out the motion of the door. I stopped walking around and sat on the bed — the door continued to move. It started moving again after a short pause. In a minute or two it stopped. I attempted to restart the movements of the door by walking up and down, but there was no movement. I even tried stomping on the floor, but the door remained still.

Debbie went to bed early and she said she felt someone sit on the edge of bed while she had been alone. She had consumed a tall glass of wine with dinner and I put the odd feeling on the effects of the wine.

I went to bed about midnight, sleeping on the side of the bed that faced the door of the narrow room. I was very tired from a long day. I found myself unable to sleep in the strange bed. I glanced up toward the door and, in the dim light that filtered into the third floor room, I saw a jet black form. It appeared in the doorway. It just stood for moment, its arms hanging down at its sides. I couldn't see a face on the form. It seemed almost like a shadow. After several seconds it moved to the left and vanished. It seemed to be a man. Debbie who was exhausted, was fast asleep. There was no sound. Could it have been the ghost of Harry Houdini? I don't think so, but it was something out of the ordinary.

Do I feel that the Glen Tavern Inn is haunted? Yes! I have seen something there that I can't explain that confirms the idea that the old hotel does have phantom residents.

The La Conchita Hauntings

Between Ventura and Carpinteria, on the coastline is a unique small community called La Conchita, Today it is best known for the unique, banana plantation where experimental breeds of this tropical fruit are grown. La Conchita has a long history of ghostly events. Several of the older homes have their resident spirits, and phantoms of dark ladies are said to wander the streets at night.

The house on Santa Barbara Avenue appears normal enough. For the family that moved in nothing seemed out of the ordinary—at least not at first. The daughter was the first to see them. She saw people, average looking people walking around the outside of the house and looking in the windows at all hours of the day and night. The images were of older men and women which would abruptly vanish away into nothingness. It seemed as if they were looking for someone or something. Frightened, the family asked around the small community and learned that others living on that street had also seen ghosts. That was before the strange events began to happen inside the house! First it was the sound of footsteps in the hallway, then the unmistakable whispering in rooms that were unoccupied. Then, one morning they went into the living room and saw a blanket on the floor with what looked like a body under it. The daughter remember that the form was "like a mummy" with the blanket tightly tucked in around the human-like shape. They pulled the blanket away and there was nothing under it! Asking around with some of the "Old Timers" they discovered that two decades ago a group of what were described as "Hippies" rented the house. The group, so it was said, were members of a Satanic Cult who performed elaborate rituals in the house. Perhaps, in there attempts to practice satanic magic they inadvertently opened a portal into another world, a door that was still ajar unleashing supernatural forces. The family moved away but the house still stands on Santa Barbara Avenue. Perhaps the portal has at last closed and the present residents have at last put to rest the wandering ghosts.

One ghostly event took place several years ago, and was told to me by one of my students in a class on ghost hunting I offer at the Ventura Community College in Ventura. The students often share their accounts with me, knowing they will not be held up to ridicule or scorn.

"This occurrence involved my parents one winter evening north of the La Conchita beach community. They decided to do a little surf fishing at one of their favorite spots, which was across from where the banana farm is now located. After getting the fishing gear and bait divided up, my mother moved about twenty yards away from where my father was standing.

It was the time of evening just before it got completely dark when my father sensed someone standing behind him. He tuned, looked around and didn't see anyone. Suddenly, he felt two short puffs of air blown at the back of his neck. Again, he looked around and there was no one there. The only thing he noticed was my mother's silhouette a few yards down the beach. Still, he sensed someone behind him. He moved a few feet to one side and again two short puffs of air hit the back of his neck. This continued for about fifteen minutes at different intervals. No matter which way he moved he would feel the puffs of air.

On the way home, my mother asked who he was speaking with. She told him she glanced over and saw an outline of a person behind him and she looked again and the person was gone. Then my father told her what had happened. The day after, two kids were hiking around, and discovered a partially decomposed body directly across the highway from where my parents were fishing."

The Haunting of the Cristy Ranch, Santa Cruz Island

Fog haloed the white and yellow buildings, enshrouding them with an air of mystery. Perhaps it was the silence that gave the place an unsettling feeling, a haunted silence. I had been asked to fly to the remote Cristy Ranch on Santa Cruz Island, in the Santa Barbara Channel, to investigate rumors of a haunted room where a lady in green is said to wander. I requested that room in hopes of witnessing a psychic event. I would not be disappointed!

The flight over the blue waters to the island provided a spectacular view of the channel and landing on the dirt airstrip was as thrilling as any of the rides at Disneyland. Most of the passengers on the plane were simply vacationers planning a weekend of hiking, snorkeling, fishing, and relaxing. For me, this was a classic example of a workman's holiday, collecting data on a suspected haunted site.

The ranch, located about a mile from the airstrip, loomed out of the fog; two large buildings painted white and yellow. Both of the structures were well over a hundred years old and both built of adobe. Few ghosts are reported in the older 1860 period house. Most paranormal activity is centered in the 1888 bunk house on the second floor.

Climbing the wooden stairs, I made my way to the haunted room. The wooden boards creaked as I entered. Small and spartan, the room seemed to have an atmosphere all its own. This would be my home for the next few days and nights. I hoped the phantom lady would make her presence known to confirm the reports. If she failed to show up, the rumors would remain unconfirmed.

Today the Christy ranch is operated as a resort, they offer tours and an out of the way vacation for those who wish to get away from it all in a natural setting. It was during these tours that stories of the ghostly lady began to surface. It was this as well as other strange events that led the group to

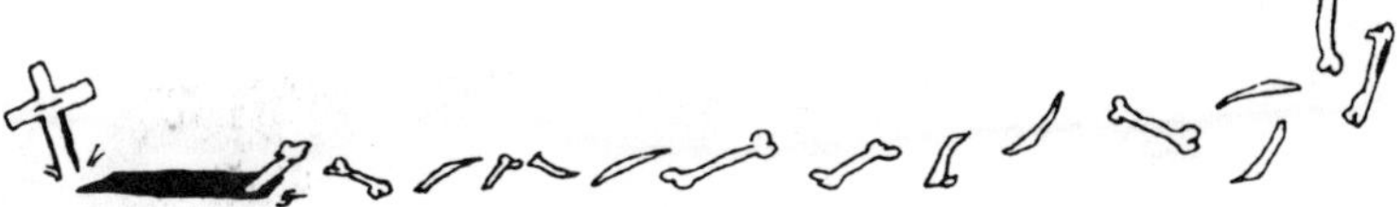

request my services. I questioned members of the staff and recorded this remarkable event. I print this only on the condition that the identity of the informant be kept confidential.

"It was . . . maybe October or September, and we had a large group of birders (bird watchers) out. They were all interested in the birds on the island; we have over 123 different types just around the ranch itself. It was on the second night of the trip, and I was mopping up the dining room, about 9:30 in the evening. I wasn't drinking that night, there never is a lot of drinking out here on the island. I had all the chairs on the table. I had just finished, stepped out for a minute, and when I came in . . . I saw a paper . . . sign spinning around and around by itself. Later I was in the kitchen talking when a whole pile of books flew off the microwave onto the floor, like some one had pushed them. Now, in the pile were books on birds, geology, Chumash Indians, all kinds of things that relate to the island. Only half of the books fell. Just then . . . I heard a deep baritone voice say: 'bird'. It came to me like flash, those are all bird books, I said. "When he collected the books from the floor, he discovered that his insight had been correct, all the books were about birds." I was kind of spooked about that," he recalls.

Others had experienced more dramatic encounters at the ranch. A staff member confided that there had once been a female cook who was staying at the house. "She woke up and felt something kneeling down, close to her face and looking at her. She couldn't breathe. She left that very day. She couldn't take it."

After gathering these accounts I was ready for anything. The first night nothing happened but the last night of the investigation, during a light rain, my stakeout reaped a ghostly reward. It was 10:58 p.m. I was sitting on the bed writing, when I glanced up at the window that faced the balcony. In the light of the lamp on the balcony I saw a dark figure glide past the window down the balcony! A sudden chill raced down my spine, for the dark form made no sound.

It could not have been a real person as the wooden balcony creaks under the slightest weight. I jumped up and looked into the darkness and rain, there was no one there! By comparing the dark shape to the window I determined that the apparition was about five feet two inches in height. This compared well with other sightings that described a short figure. But who is the ghost and why does he or she haunt? I determined that only a seance would unravel the mystery.

After interviewing those who have experienced psychic phenomena at the historic ranch I had to admit something hovered about the site. The visitors and staff gathered in the dining room of the 1888 adobe bunk house, with candles flickering. A circle was formed and the medium went into a deep trance, a self-induced hypnotic state that enables the "spirits" to use the medium as a channel of communication. The following excerpts were taken from the tape recording of the seance. I was ably assisted by Mrs. Laurie Hunt, who was making a television documentary on the Cristy Ranch Resort. Her help and background as a journalist were a valuable asset to the investigation.

After several moments the medium began to speak.

(Laurie): "Is there someone there?"

(Medium): "Yes"

(Laurie): "What is your name?"

(Medium): "Mary"

(Laurie): "Mary?"

(Medium): "Mary Morrison Reese"

(Laurie): "Did you live here on the island?"

(Medium): "No"

(Laurie): "Where did you live?"

(Medium): "SEATTLE"

(Laurie): "Why are you here?"

(Medium): "Daniel, my husband."

(Laurie): "Why?"

(Medium): "Because of what he did."

(Laurie): "What did he do?"

(Medium): "He's a murderer."

(Laurie): "Your husband is a murderer? Who did he

murder?"

(Medium): "Thousands, hundreds."

(Laurie): "How?"

(Medium): "He threw them into the sea. To rob them."

(Laurie): "Where did he do this?"

(Medium): "In the channel. He was to drop them at Ortega Beach. He robbed them and threw them into the sea."

(Laurie): "When?"

(Medium): "1847."

(Laurie): "Were you there?"

(Medium): "I was on the ship."

(Laurie): "Did you try to stop him?"

(Medium): "Yes, I told him it was wrong. He said they were heathens. They were Chinese. It didn't matter, and he killed them."

(Laurie): "So, why did you come to tell us?"

(Medium): "I threw myself off the ship. I fell into the sea. Now I am here, I'm here."

(Laurie): "What are you wearing?"

(Medium): "A dress."

(Laurie): "A red dress, a green dress?"

(Medium): "Yes, it was so terrible. They went in two at a time, tied together. They were thrown from the stern. They had brought them up from the hold. They took everything they had. Hundreds of dollars."

(Laurie): "What was the name of your ship?"

(Medium): "Ellen."

(Laurie): "Where did she come from?"

(Medium): "Seattle."

(Laurie): "Where was it going?"

(Medium): "Los Angeles, San Pedro. They brought the Chinese. Picked them from off a ship."

(Laurie): "What happened to your husband?"

(Medium): "He was killed at sea. Accident."

(Laurie): "What happened to the ship?"

(Medium): "Lost off of Hawaii. But I was not there."

(Laurie): "Why do you come back here?"

(Medium): "For his sin. The sin on his soul."

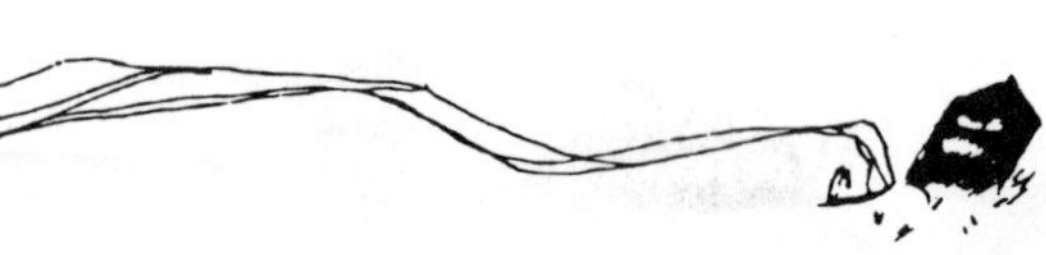

(Laurie): "Why do you have to pay for his sins?"

(Medium): "Because he will not. I told him it was wrong."

(Laurie): "Why do you come to the island? Not the channel?"

(Medium): "My body came here with those of the Chinese. I fell with them into the sea."

(Laurie): "What do you want?"

(Medium): "Prayers, prayers for my husband."

(Laurie): "Why do you want prayers for a murderer?"

(Medium): "So he will not burn in HELL. I fear that I too will burn for I watched and did nothing."

(Laurie): "You tried to stop him."

(Medium): "When it became unbearable. Two hundred people died."

(Laurie): "Did other people know of this?"

(Medium): "Only the crew. In Seattle they thought we carried lumber. But we did not."

(Laurie): "Would we find remains? Would there be a place we could find remains to prove your story?"

(Medium): "I do not know. I came here with the others. To hell he said and I went over the side. They turned the ship but it was too late. The heads bobbed up and down, Chinese families, they went under the waves one at a time."

(Laurie): "Where are you when you are not here?"

(Medium): "At the beach. Looking for the ship. It will come back someday. It will have two masts. It will come back for me and the others. What shall I do? Could you have a mass said for me?"

(Laurie): "By who?"

(Medium): "A priest. No one ever said a mass for me."

(Laurie): "We will ask someone to say a mass for you and take your guilt away."

(Medium): "Thank you. Maybe my soul will burn clean in purgatory."

Is the lady in green the sad spectre of Mary Morrison Reese? Perhaps her guilt holds her earthbound to this one location and our seance may help to lift the suffering of this lady. Research may uncover the ship Ellen or its cruel

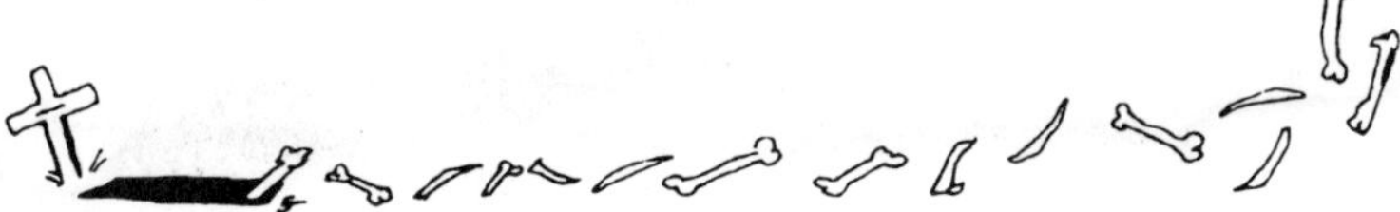

Captain Daniel Reese and until then the identity of the
phantom must remain a mystery.

A week after the visit to the island I developed the photographs I had taken of the two adobe buildings and the scenic
wonders of the west end of Santa Cruz Island. When I
examined the photographs I saw a figure in one print, the
figure was in my room! It resembled a woman in a grey
dress! She is seen in the doorway of the room. Was it a ghost
trying further communication?

Summerland Ghosts

South of Santa Barbara lies the picturesque seaside community called Summerland. Few know it is a community designed by ghosts! Today it's best known as an area inhabited by artists and creative people, or as the nude beach of Santa Barbara. The few who have studied its unique history know its links to spiritualism.

The town was founded in 1883 by Mr. H.L. Williams as a place where spiritualists could practice their unique brand of religion, un-hampered by undue skepticism. Spiritualism holds that the dead do not die and that, with the help of gifted individuals called mediums they can and do communicate with the living. Fascinated with this new religion, Mr. Williams planned his new community with spiritualism in mind. The streets were given names that relate to the new faith. Lillie Avenue, the main street today of the small town, is a popular spiritual symbol. The unfolding pedals of the lily reflecting the spiritual unfolding of the soul. The name of the community is that of the lowest of the seven spheres (or heavens) of classical spiritualism.

Long ago the community was called "Spooksville." Some of the old timers openly state that every other old house in Summerland is haunted! When the houses were built by spiritualist carpenters, they incorporated occult symbols into the rafters and walls. These occult elements make them accessible to spirits and ghosts. The early spiritualists first erected a large building to use as a church. This was called "Liberty Hall" by the members. Others referred to it as "Spook Hall." Here the devoted held their elaborate seances, inviting well-known mediums and lecturers to hold services. It was planned that a retirement home for old mediums would be built. Also planned was a large library to meet the needs of a very literate and well-educated population.

The idealistic community succumbed to the hands of greed when oil was accidently discovered by a resident trying to dig a water well. The discovery of "black gold" forever altered the history and face of Summerland. The spiritualist dominance declined as oil-men and capitalists moved in to harvest the new-found wealth. A small group did hold out until the old spiritualist church was demolished to make way for the freeway. But ghosts are not subject to earthly laws and the sighting of phantoms is a common occurrence in the beachside community.

The Big Yellow House Restaurant in Summerland has been the best known haunted site in the town for a number of years. The ghost, nicknamed "Hector," has been written about in various books and magazines. He has many a trick to surprise a young waitress or a sensitive guest. Some believe Hector is a "dirty old man" ghost because he focuses his attention on attractive young women. Some have even accused him of an occasional pinch on the bottom, certainly an earthy way for a spirit to behave. The ghost is so popular that the story of Hector was once printed on the cover of the menu. There is some evidence that the Big Yellow House was used to hold seances long ago. Perhaps the playful Hector is simply a left over spirit from one of those lively gatherings of a century past. He is one of three ghosts some say reside at the popular restaurant. A guest visiting the restaurant needed to use the rest room and, with her husband waiting she ducked into the bathroom. There she saw a woman dressed in a blue dress standing to one side glaring at her in anger. She seem to be in her late sixties, and dressed in the style of the turn of the century. The visitor thought that the aged woman must be an actress in a costume from a local play company and tried to ignore her. She was gone when the woman left the stall yet she hadn't heard the door open or close. When she rejoined her husband, who was standing by the door to the bathroom, she asked if he had seen the oddly dressed lady—He said he had not—in fact no one had entered or left while she was in the bathroom . Others having a simple dinner in the elegant mansion have felt a strange coldness envelope then when they dine on the second floor. Most of the manifestations have been reported in what was once the old library. During a seance held in the room years ago, a tape recorder used to document the event was tossed across the room by an unseen force. A team of parapsychologists from UCLA spent a night in the place with sensitive equipment. They recorded enough information to deem the hauntings genuine.

The Tidepool Reflections Shop, on Lillie Avenue, sells seashells and tee-shirts to the passing tourists. Few realize that the old building was once haunted. The owner and manager, Ms. Betty Migneron, tells of misty figures seen when they first moved into the building and that objects moved about on their own. They were plagued by these spectres until a patron, who is a Spiritualist, offered to "give the house a blessing." Since that day the ghost of the shell shop has been quiet.

KTMS Radio personality Tom Carrol is well known for his quick wit and ability to "think on his feet," but he hadn't reckoned with ghosts before he moved into an old house on Lillie Avenue in Summerland. He recounts how a package of cigarettes vanished from his house after he spoke of quitting smoking. Another time his favorite pair of brown shoes vanished, only to reappear three days later, freshly polished, with shoe trees in them, in the center of his closet where he had looked a dozen times or more. He has heard a number of odd sounds in the old house, and believes it might be the spirit of a woman, perhaps a former resident, who as a believer in the doctrine of spiritualism, has not passed away but continues to watch after the old home. These are but a few of the many stories of hauntings that can be found in the small community built for ghosts.

Does the Ghost of Ronald Coleman Haunt Montecito?

It is a simple stone; black marble. It stands on a low hill facing the Pacific Ocean, in the picturesque Santa Barbara Cemetery. It is the tombstone of actor Ronald Coleman. It bears this inscription from Shakespear's The Tempest;

"Our revels are now ended. These our actors, as I foretold you, were all spirits, and are melted into air, into thin air; and, like the base-less fabric of this vision, the cloud clapped towers, the gorgeous palaces, the solemn temples, the great globe itself, yea, all which we inherit, shall dissolve and like this insubstantial pageant faded, leave not a track behind. We are such stuff as dreams are made of. And our little life is rounded with sleep."

Few know that this talented British born actor was a resident and popular innkeeper in Santa Barbara and is buried in the community cemetery. In life Coleman, known to his many friends and family as 'Ronnie', loved the beauty of the South Coast. The happiest years of his life were spent in this corner of the world — but could it be that his love was so deep that it continued after the transition some call death?

Mrs. Patricia S. had always loved Ronald Coleman ever since the night she first saw Lost Horizon on a flickering black and white television three decades ago. Having learned that the actor is buried in Santa Barbara she made a special trip there to place a single rose upon his grave. She drove around the large cemetery several times, lost and unable to find the grave. For some reason she found herself silently asking the "spirit" where the grave is located. She once again started to drive and went right to it.

She reverently approached the stone, thanked him for all the entertainment he has given her over the years in his many films. Patricia placed the rose on the grave and left.

That night she had a remarkable dream. A vivid dream in color. In the dream she found herself at a great party with

lots of music and dancing. At the party she met Ronald Coleman. Smiling, he thanked her for the rose and they talked for some time. He told about his life and the many good times he had in Hollywood. She woke from the dream with a complete feeling of peace. The feeling lasted a day and a half. Was it a dream, or was it something else?

Ronald Coleman owned the popular San Ysidro Ranch in Montecito, and made the place his second home. He loved being an innkeeper, and frequently spent time with guests at the restaurant and thirty-eight cottages. Guests included some of the crowned heads of filmdom — Rex Harrison, Merle Oberon and Vivian Leigh. John and Jackie Kennedy spent their honeymoon there. Other notable guests included Sir Winston Churchill, Bertrand Russel, Aldous Huxley, and legend states that John Galsworthy revised his The Forsyte Saga in the Outlook Cottage.

Ronald Coleman's residence was complete with an art studio for his paintings. Few of his fans realize that Coleman was an accomplished artist.

Though the San Ysidro Ranch never made money, Coleman always told friends that it was his happiest investment.

In 1958, Ronnie peacefully passed over to that land where all mortals travel in their time. But, some say in hushed voices that he visits his old ranch, 'just to see how things are going.' Some who have visited the bar tell of bottles moving by themselves, bottles of expensive scotch, the same kind favored by Ronnie in life. Others speak of doors opening and closing by themselves and shadows moving in the restaurant. Still others tell of encountering the smiling figure of the actor, still greeting his guests and making sure that everyone is treated like a personal friend. Local historian Maggie Monroe, assistant director of the Santa Barbara Historical museum has collected a number of ghostly tales linked to Santa Barbara County. She grew up in the Montecito area and related to me the story of a ghost said to haunt the building that houses the San Ysidro restaurant. During the turn of the century large groups of Chinese workers were used on the ranch. One of the Chinese was known as a clever fellow and set himself up a nice room in the unused attic of the stone house. He turned the space into a comfortable apartment much better than the humble barracks the rest of the Chinese works 'had to make do with'. One of the Chinese grew jealous and in his anger burned the building down! The Chinese man in the attic was burned to death. They say that the cooks and bartenders have encounter the ghost of the Chinese man. He seems a helpful specter and the kitchen staff refer to him as "just another member of the crew."

The essence of Coleman is firmly established at the old inn, and his memory will be a part of it forever. Perhaps the reported sightings are simply wishful thinking; the collective desire to meet such a charming and graceful gentleman. Perhaps they are real encounters with something beyond our understanding — something that hints that life doesn't stop at the grave. Who can say for certain?

The Ghost of Brinkerhoff Avenue

The woman was convinced that she had seen a ghost. Her eyes were wide and a tremble came to her voice as she recalled the encounter with the ghost of Santa Barbara's Brinkerhoff Avenue.

"I saw him walking towards me . . . he was wearing a black coat and a small bow tie," She recalled, "He didn't look right, his skin was terribly white, almost as if he was wearing stage makeup . . . he looked right at me and walked past me. I felt an icy chill go down my arms as he passed to the left of me. I turned and he vanished!" The encounter took place on the short one block street named for Dr. Samuel Brinkerhoff, Santa Barbara's first American doctor.

It is located between Chapala and De La Vina streets, just off State Street. It is a neighborhood that would make a spirit feel right at home. Both sides of the street are lined with Victorian homes all built before 1916. Today Brinkerhoff Avenue is known for its many antique shops housed in the historic residences. Though the owners of the shops claim they haven't seen the ghost, most of them know the story of "Lord Harry."

His real name was Harry Hawcroft, English by nationality, a blacksmith by trade. A very popular man, he always wore a bow tie and white shirts with pearl buttons. Because of his seemingly odd ways and distinct accent, the locals called him "Lord Harry." He lived at the 1889 house at 519 Brinkerhoff. Today the decorative house with its fish scale shingles and stained glass windows is not open to the public. It is decorated with odds and ends from historic gas stations. The present owner buys and sells items linked to the early petroleum industry.

They were the ones to first experience the ghost of "Lord Harry." While remodeling the house, odd things started to happen, work was done by unseen hands. Sheets of plywood were nailed into place by a phantom carpenter. The owner investigated the history of the house, and came across a 19th century photograph of Harry Hawcroft wearing his blacksmith's apron and his distinctive bow tie. Once a houseguest came down to the kitchen and saw the spectre standing there in the clothing of last century — as she watched, he vanished away into nothingness. Items that were missing, including a winning lottery ticket, appeared on the dining table, along with valuable earrings that had been lost.

If the new sightings are accurate, the ghost of "Lord Harry" has taken to strolling the lane in the early evening. A woman who has a history of psychic encounters has felt his presence walking near the ornate house at 528 Brinkerhoff. "I could feel his presence." She stated. "He wants us to know that he still watches out over the street."

Still another sighting, this time by a young man driving down the street at about 6:30 in November, 1992, claimed that the dark figure stepped out in front of his car. He braked as the man just stood there looking at the driver. "I saw his lips move but I couldn't hear what he was saying," the driver said. "Then he just faded out. He melted into the darkness of the street."

Records indicate that he was a volunteer fireman. Perhaps he is still watching over his neighborhood; still keeping an eye out for fires. Who can say for sure? But if you should find yourself on one-block-long Brinkerhoff Avenue, and you should see a man wearing a dark coat and bow tie — look again, for it may well be the wandering ghost of "Lord Harry."

Where the Walls Sing: Mission La Purisima, Lompoc

"I've heard lots of different things," said the park ranger at Mission La Purisima. "The tale of a monk who walks through the gardens in the mornings and evenings. The horseman who rides at night. The bricks falling down in certain portions of the various rooms. We've had people complain of cold spots, very frigid areas at times when they shouldn't be. It moves around. Whatever is here, it moves to different rooms at different times. People ask about rooms like the Cartel. We have a couple of people here who will not lock up the Cartel. They are afraid of the Cartel because of things they have felt. I've felt apprehensive at times and yet I confronted my feelings and made friends (with the ghosts). That's a nice way to be. Someone felt something in the library."

For generations legends of ghosts have circulated around the old Spanish Mission at Lompoc. Tales of a bandit's mounted ghost, murdered vaquero's phantom and spectral robed monks have been told for many decades. These stories and accounts of real sightings continue to happen at the restored mission. These accounts drew a team of psychic investigators to conduct a number of simple experiments to try to discover the nature of ghosts said to wander the mission.

The team experienced the most profound event in the padre's chapel, where they heard mission era songs of the mass. The building is equipped with a tape player, and they assumed it was the taped music. They were surprised to learn the tape system was broken. Steve Jones, the park ranger confirmed this. "I physically checked it as early as ... 1:30 (or) 2:00. I was right outside the church and noticed the music wasn't playing. But I had something else to attend to. It's a reel to reel tape, magnetic leader on each side, so it reads the magnetic leader and plays backwards and goes back the other way. The magnetic leader at one end is broken . . . there is no way that tape could have been playing."

There were a number of odd things about the music the team reported hearing. Mr. C.L. a retired law enforcement officer heard the music in the chapel. "Most indubitably! I'm not a Catholic, I thought it was a mass. There was instrumentation, but there were no voices in the background and I couldn't distinguish anything that was being said and wasn't really trying to. First thing, that insistence by the ranger that there was no music in the church . . . but I know there was. It was very clear, not any imagination, and I was sure it was just a mass. It wasn't the same one that I heard last week, it was not the same, I'm sure. But I heard it, it was there!"

Ms. M.F. heard the music. "I went to the window, and it was really loud. It sounded like singing and choir music. It was weird. It wasn't organ music, it was like guitars and flutes and that type of thing. Then I stuck my face to the window. As soon as I looked into the window, it stopped."

Mrs. J.L.'s account depicted how different people heard different things. "Later, at about 4:15 p.m., I went into the second chapel by myself. When I walked in, I heard very soft church music. It was very pleasing and reminded me of my childhood days. At this point I walked over to the altar, knelt down and just watched the church. I felt very nostalgic and peaceful. Just then Diana walked in and we continued to tour the church. We walked into the back room and Diana began complaining how loud the music was, and it was giving her a headache. I though that was because she was psychic, she couldn't concentrate because of the music. At no time did I think the music was loud. I considered it very peaceful. We then left and went to other the areas of the mission. Two hours later we were together with the class when we learned that the music recorder was broken. Yet everyone heard the music!"

Ms. L.S. recounted her experience "I heard music. It was a musical, melody-kind of sound. I don't know how to explain it. Way down at the end of this corridor. I felt cold spots and clammy. I know what cold breezes are like but this was

totally different. I have never felt anything like this."

Mr. K.C. also heard the spectral music. "I heard music around at the front of the building. It was lousy, like woodwinds, I don't know. I heard music, it was real loud."

Other events took place in other parts of the mission. Mrs. J.L. heard voices. "While walking through the weaving room and entering the court yard, I heard some male voices. I only heard about two sentences and could not make out what they were saying. It sounded low, like the mumbled chants I have heard watching cowboy and Indian movies. I sat on the ledge hoping that I might hear some more, and was then interrupted by fellow classmates and the voices stopped. This was about 4:00 p.m."

The team came away convinced that something does indeed inhabit the place. The supernatural is commonplace there. They heard singing in empty rooms, they heard guitars when no one was present and felt odd cold spots on warm summer days. La Purisima is indeed a haunted place!

If you seek ghosts or wish to wander where ghosts walk, do visit the Mission La Purisima. Find a quiet place on the vast grounds and relax. Close your eyes and listen, the voices of the past might be heard on the wind, or perhaps a lonely Chumash Indian flute, or maybe the songs of the mass, long silent. At La Purisima this world and the next seem very close and a chance encounter with a spirit, somehow natural.

A strange event happened in the chapel of the Mission several months after the investigation had concluded. A special event was held where a musician was performing, playing a guitar, at the altar of the church. The man was singing and playing to the group, walking back and forth. At one point he stepped upon the grave of Padre Mariano Payeras, buried near the altar, and at that moment his guitar went out of tune! The musician had to stop and, stepping to one side, he re-tuned his instrument. It took several moments, but at last he could continue his performance. Once again he stepped upon the grave and once again the guitar went completely out of tune!

Ghosts Haunt the Popular Los Olivos Tavern

The psychic felt the presence when she first walked into the historic Mattie's Tavern Restaurant in the quaint village of Los Olivos, five miles north of Solvang.

"There is a man here," she said with a whisper, "I see a man with whiskers, white whiskers. He lived here."

She felt his presence as she and her husband enjoyed a fine steak dinner in the rustic surroundings of the inn.

The icy phantom's presence seemed to have been forgotten as they enjoyed the evening, until she looked up and turned white. Her eyes wide, she began to shake. Concerned, her husband asked what was wrong.

"It's a woman with a white dress," she said in a low voice. "Can't you see her? She is there by the door." The man peered into the dim light but could see nothing. "She died long ago - when this place was a hotel. She died of poison. I think she took her own life — before the turn of the century. She is so sad. She wants something. There is something missing here that she wants."

The psychic couldn't stay for dessert. She paid the bill and drove into the night. For three days the psychic was troubled by nightmares of the strange woman and her untimely end. She saw the narrow rooms with the simple furniture. The night stand and the lamp. She saw the bitter white powder that the woman took with wine. She felt the pain of her slow death. Why had she taken her own life?

The husband returned to the inn and asked if there were any stories of ghosts or the supernatural events at the historic tavern. A waitress said that things had been moved around. She didn't say what had happened in the saloon of the inn.

The tavern was built by Swiss immigrant Felix Mattie in 1886 and named the Central Hotel. At that time Los Olivos was the terminus of a narrow gauge railroad, and Felix Mattie saw this as a place to build a business. He specialized in the restaurant part of his hotel, developing a reputation for gourmet dinners. Even when a newer and larger hotel was

constructed two years later, Mattie was so well established that the new hotel could only take his overflow. When the new hotel burned, Mattie expanded and renamed his establishment the "Hotel Los Olivos."

Violence was no stranger to the tavern. In 1891 a lynch mob attacked the inn when they learned that two suspected murderers where being held by the local sheriff. The mob stormed the inn. The prisoners managed to escape dressed as women.

In 1930, Felix Mattie died. In his honor, the establishment was renamed Mattie's Tavern. From the day of his death rumors began to surface that Mattie was walking the hotel that he so dearly loved in life. Whatever the identity of the ghost, the atmosphere of the old inn seems to be charged with the essence of the Old West.

Today the place is managed by the Chart House enterprise chain of steak houses. Who knows, maybe Felix still watches over the inn that bears his name.

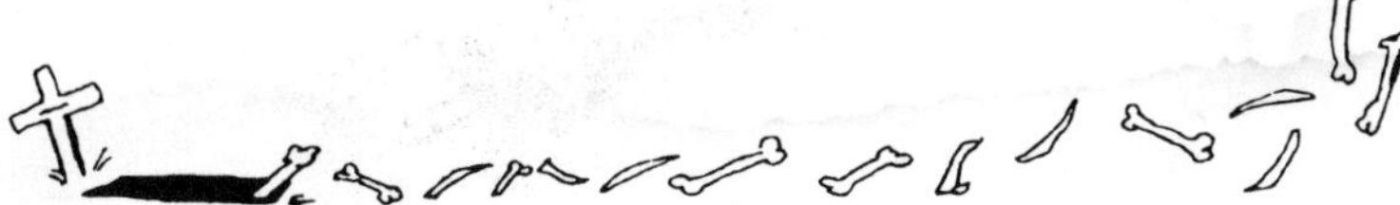

Santa Maria Seance

The historic Santa Maria Inn has stood for elegance and style in Santa Maria since it first opened its doors in 1917. But, rumors began to circulate several years ago that the graceful Inn was harboring a persistent phantom resident, referred to by the staff as the "Captain."

During the renovation of the Inn two people stayed in room 103. They told of waking up at night, between the hours of one and three hearing doors open and close and people walking down the hallways. When they checked, there was no one there and the hotel was secured for the night. After the Inn was re-opened after renovation one of the gardeners saw the image of a man standing on one of the landings of the outside stairways. The gardener thought it was one of the guests until it vanished away into nothingness. The man walked into the Inn as white as a sheet and said, " I just saw the captain." A former assistant manager, Mr. Rodney Jones told of several experiences he had in the old Inn. He said that the curtains in room 216 sometimes bilowed by themselves— even when the windows were closed! A member of the company that manages the Inn today confided that, "He (The Captain) is all around the place".

On September 3, 1989, a group of ghost hunters led by psychic Debbie Christenson Senate and I checked into the Santa Maria Inn to investigate the rumors, in an attempt to determine if the Inn was really haunted. For twenty-four hours we wandered the halls, performed a number of experiments, and questioned the staff about the mysterious "Captain." Debbie agreed to act as medium in our experiment. At midnight, in the room where a majority of the psychic experiences have been reported, we gathered to conduct a seance in an attempt to communicate with the spectre.

The medium slumped forward in her chair. In the dim light her face seemed to relax, then it became contorted with pain.

(Richard): "Who are you?"

(Debbie): "Who am I?"

(Richard): "Who are you?"
(Debbie): "Peppy."
(Richard): "Peppy? Are you Mexican?"
(Debbie): "No silly, it's my name."
(Richard): "Peppy is a Mexican name isn't it?"
(Debbie): "No, it's my name. Are you waiting for me?"
(Richard): "Who are you waiting for?"
(Debbie): "I am waiting for the limousine that WR is sending for me."
(Richard): "Who is WR? Is he your husband?"
(Debbie): "WR is Mr. Hearst, silly."
(Richard): "You know Mr. Hearst?"
(Debbie): "Yes very well."
(Richard): "What year is it?"
(Debbie): "1935."
(Richard): "Do you often go to Hearst's Castle?"
(Debbie): "To the ranch. I often travel with my aunt."
(Richard): "Aunt? Who is your aunt?"
(Debbie): "Marion."
(Richard): "Did you work for Mr. Hearst?"
(Debbie): "Once."
(Richard): "What did you do for Mr. Hearst?"
(Debbie): "In London I worked for one of his magazines as a writer."
(Richard): "Peppy? What kind of name is that?"
(Debbie): "I was called Peppy because I was always peppy."
(Richard): "Did you stay at the castle much?"
(Debbie): "I spent a lot of time at the ranch. I use to stay over at the Casa Del Mar."
(Richard): "What is the Casa Del Mar?"
(Debbie): "I'm cold, I'm cold. Do you have any coke?"
(Richard): "Coke? Do you want a Coca-Cola?"
(Debbie): "No silly, coke. I need some real bad. I'm cold."
(Richard): "Cold?"
(Debbie): "Yes, I want it now!"
(Richard): "What do you want to do with coke?"
(Debbie): "I take it."

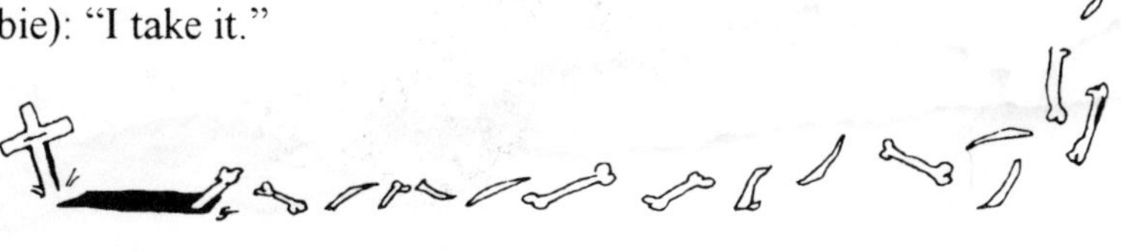

(Richard): "Take it? You mean cocaine?"
(Debbie): "Yes. Coke, uppies."
(Richard): "You took drugs?"
(Debbie): "For my sinuses. Are they here yet?"
(Richard): "Did you telephone them?"
(Debbie): "Yes, I know they forgave me. Hasn't the car arrived yet?"
(Richard): "Why did they need to forgive you? What did you do to Mr. Hearst?"
(Debbie): "Get me some coke. Please get me some."
(Richard): "What happened? Why did you start taking cocaine?"
(Debbie): "I was sick. Alma used to give it to me."
(Richard): "Who is Alma?"
(Debbie): "You know Alma, Alma Rubens. She used to live upstairs from me in New York."
(Richard): "You acquired coke from her?"
(Debbie): "Yes, I've got to go now."
(Richard): "Did you stay at the Santa Maria Inn?"
(Debbie): "Yes, I'm sorry but I have to go now. Do you see the limousine?"
(Richard): "Peppy why do you have to go?"
(Debbie): No response
(Richard): "Peppy?"
(Debbie): No response

The team had expected to receive information on a mysterious "Captain," and instead communicated with a young cocaine addict. Research is still underway to identify if such an individual with the name of "Peppy" lived, and if so, if she was in some way related to Marion Davies, William Randolph Hearst's mistress.

Researchers at the Hearst Castle State Park did say that a sister to Marion may have had that nickname. They did confirm that there is a Casa Del Mar and it was the guest house most used by the Hearst and Davies families. There was an actress named Alma Rubens who did work for the Hearst film company. She was a confirmed drug addict and died of an overdose in the mid 1930's. Still, research may

someday prove or disprove the existence of "Peppy." Does she still walk the halls of Santa Maria Inn waiting for the limousine to take her on to Hearst Castle? Or did the phantom car arrive, at long last, to transport the weary soul to a heavenly Hearst Castle, where all is as it should be and WR still holds court over his estate in the clouds?

The team recorded several odd events in their ghost hunt, but none were conclusive. Some of the team members recorded a number of odd events. Ora Philips stated that, "In front of room 144 I felt a distinct chill." Diane Erdelyis recalled that. "During the seance I felt a jolt under the table. The lights in the seance room flickered and pulsated." Edward Jackson remembered that, "I was taking a shower and reached for the bar of soap and it moved. It just floated across the room." One couple heard footsteps in their room and several heard knocks and raps late at night. The rumors of ghosts remain, but the evidence is lacking to prove that the historic Inn is indeed haunted.

The Ghost of John Vittey Haunts this Old House

The cook ran out of the kitchen of the San Luis Obispo restaurant with his eyes popping out of their sockets. He was new. He hadn't heard about the resident ghost, but he had seen him, an opaque white figure drifting through the wall of the walk-in freezer in the back of the kitchen.

Built as a home in 1917, when the land was part of the Bishop Dairy, at the foot of Bishop's peak, the house was converted into a restaurant in 1950. When it first opened to the public there was only one meal on the menu, fried chicken and potatoes. The place slowly attracted a following of local ranchers and cowboys, as well as a reputation as a rowdy place for a drink. It was in the early years that the first rumors of a ghost are thought to have started. Renamed "This Old House" after a popular song, the place prospered and additions were made to the old ranch house.

Visitors and waitresses over the years claimed to have felt something out of the ordinary in one of the old rooms — a place were there is a strange coldness.

Manager Marsha Fischleck once said: " . . . a lot of us have noticed a cool wind . . . you know . . . like when someone walks real close to you and you can feel the air move . . . only, well, there is no one there."

Psychic researcher Brian Cloniger visited the haunted restaurant and interviewed one of the staff members. She believed that the "middle room" was where the person who is the ghost lived and perhaps died. One of the waitresses, recently interviewed, told of feeling someone or something "brush past them" in that one small section of the room.

The bar has its own set of spirits. Once, a glass placed close to the edge of an upper shelf was seen to move under its own power. It didn't fall right down — rather it was seen to fly off at a 45 degree angle to land among some bottles without breaking one of them. This took place without a

strong wind or an earth tremor.

The offices of the restaurant are also haunted. Twelve years ago one of the managers was working one warm afternoon at his desk. He looked up from his paperwork and was surprised to see the figure of a hazy, misty man standing there just looking at him. He glanced away for a moment, and when he looked up the apparition had vanished.

The kitchen also has its stories, with shadowy forms drifting across the walls and the phantom sounds of pots and pans banging about, as if preparing food in the kitchen.

Several years ago one of the past owners, through the use of a Ouija Board (not an accurate tool) tried to communicate with the ghost. The pointer spelled out the name of the haunt; a Mr. John Vittey of Autry, Utah. The ghost is reported to have made his presence known by moving chairs, moaning, causing lights to flash and generally making a good-natured pest of himself.

If you ever wish to have dinner in an authentic haunted house, and if you should find yourself near San Luis Obispo with a hunger for barbecued spare ribs, look no further than THIS OLD HOUSE RESTAURANT. Try to get a seat in the old section of the building, and be sure to ask the staff about "John" and what he has been up to now. As you move about in the atmospheric restaurant keep on the alert for the sudden icy chill of a moving cold spot or the slight breeze of a passing phantom. Who knows, you may well experience something way out of the ordinary.

Adventures in a Haunted Cemetery

From time to time individuals who have read my columns, books or have taken classes that I offer, form small amateur ghost hunting groups, seeking out evidence of paranormal activity. Most of the time such gatherings find nothing but a few shivers. But every once in awhile a group will stumble onto something truly out of the ordinary. One group in the Pismo Beach area had such an encounter in a haunted cemetery and wrote me of their midnight adventures.

" ... The site referred to was the Adelaida Cemetery; (featured in my book Ghosts of the Haunted Coast) the "We" is a little ghost hunting band we formed based mainly on your books. "We" consist of myself and another young lady and her husband, and my sister. Occasionally we take friends. Myself and the young lady are both psychic to various degrees.

Our first trip to Adelaida Cemetery (north of San Luis Obispo) was in January of 1992. My sister and I made a day trip out of it. Took the kids and a picnic, etc. Our initial impressions were quiet. There was an impression of a girl with pigtails at one of the children's graves and the impression of a young wife. My sister, not me, saw the little girl with the long braids — but she saw no distinct features on the face. That was all. We assumed that since it was a quiet place in daytime, it was safe to go there at night — Wrong!

You had it right (in your book) — there is enough out in that cemetery to thrill any ghost hunter! We found out that there is nothing there on Friday nights, but there sure is on Saturday, and it is mean and angry. Our first encounter with it was frightening. I started "hearing " things screaming at me and getting visions of a wreck, blood and of all my friends dead, and me alone with them. We didn't stop at the cemetery that night to investigate. I told my sister about this and she got interested, as did her roommate. We decided to make another day of it. When we reached the cemetery the same thing showed up, and honestly, I have never felt any thing like that before, and hope never to encounter another one. It was pure concentrated EVIL. I can't stress that word enough, and it was calling to us. It wanted us to stay. I don't know why, and my psychic abilities aren't to that point yet. The thing kept following us, still calling us to stay. We made for the Old Mission at San Miguel where it left us. This thing drained me completely. We have returned several times to the site and sometimes the thing is still there. We have found plenty of spirits. The strongest spirit in the cemetery is that of a woman named Charlotte. She has shown up twice near her tombstone. I have been researching the site and have collected some bits and pieces about the place from local residents. I have heard that satanic cults practice out there. I don't know if the stories are true and I don't want to try to look them up. Dropping in on a ceremony is not high on my list of priorities."

Over and over again I have heard similar accounts of frightful phantoms, frequently described as evil, in places where satanic rituals have taken place. Many of these were reported by people who knew nothing of the history of the place and were unaware that cult rituals had been held there. The team of amateur ghost hunters, now confident that they could face evil and survive, went on to investigate the lady in black who haunts a local lake.

"We went looking for the black lady but didn't find her: we almost didn't find the lake. We did, however drive through the white lady on the road, or we think we did anyway. She was a wall of fog the length of the roadway, about five feet thick and six feet high. Just standing there in the road, on a perfectly clear night, on a nice flat stretch of road (no creek or swamp nearby). It left no water on the windshield and, as thick as it was, it should have. This didn't strike me as odd until sometime later when I was told about the white lady on the road. Not much to go on, admittedly, but enough to convince a pack of amateurs.

Arroyo Grande Ghost Hunters

Mr. Brian Cloniger, a young man who has made a hobby of researching ghosts and haunted places visited the old

Adelaida Cemetery on several occasions and each time his group encountered strange feelings and odd happenings. Once, when photographing the tombstone of Charlotte he felt something odd. He was using 35 mm camera with only one modification, a red gell was placed over the flash unit. Psychic researchers have used this to improve their chances of catching a ghost on film. When the roll of film was developed, the photograph of the ornate tombstone held an odd greenish glow hovering around the headstone!

Other groups visiting the old cemetery say that the evil of the place has grown and some say that it should be avoided at night by anyone who isn't prepared to face the negative energies said to wander the place. Some have written to me saying that anyone planning on visiting the place should come with a silver cross, Holy Water and a Bible! They should have attended church that week and be armored with faith before attempting to investigate the grounds! No one should ever visit the place alone.

My First Ghost

I didn't always believe in ghosts. In fact there was a time when I consigned such things to the funny pages. But, as they say, "seeing is believing," and when I saw a ghost I had to rethink what I believed. It wasn't the kind of thing one forgets. As any one who has experienced a ghostly sighting will tell you, it is one of the most remarkable things one can experience. Even today the image I saw is frozen in my mind's eye. I couldn't forget it if tried.

It was in the summer of 1978, at the old Spanish Mission of San Antonio de Padua, near King City, in Central California. At that time I was part of an archaeological field school being held at the mission by Dr. Bob Hoover of Cal Poly, San Luis Obispo. The team of students and archaeologists stayed at the mission, doing extensive excavations at the site of an Indian barracks that existed in the early part of the 1800s. I was not at the site long before I sensed something out of the ordinary at the place.

In some places it was as though one was being watched by unseen eyes. Late one night, after cataloging artifacts of a surface survey, I locked up the small museum and entered the vast courtyard of the mission. Like all the missions, there were flowers, gravel walkways and an ornate fountain. It was a dark and warm night; being June and in Central California, the nights can be very warm. My first goal that night was to raid the kitchen refrigerators of some cold chicken and potato salad and then go to bed. On a "dig" our days began at six a.m., so I was ready for sleep that evening. I began to walk down the gravel pathway toward the central fountain. The old mission is a dark place at night, the courtyard overpowering with the blooms of many roses and plants. The steady chirp chirp chirp of the crickets adding to the peaceful atmosphere of the place. The fountain in the courtyard constantly splashed in harmony with the insects. There the silence itself takes on its own life. Then, for some reason, the crickets stopped. The silence became somehow foreboding and haunted with speculation. It is in times like this that the thin veil that separates this world from the next seems about to rend and ghosts seem very believable indeed. It was at this point that some glint or glitter caught my eye, off to the left. I turned to observe what appeared to resemble a flame of a slowly moving candle. In the darkness it appeared as though someone was carrying a candle and walking on a parallel path and in the same direction.

As I watched the light, I seemed to notice a dark figure holding the candle. Remember that I didn't really believe in ghosts or such things. My first thought was that this was one of the team of archaeologists or perhaps a member of the monastery. Several monks still reside in the mission complex, and had proven themselves great company in the past. So, I took another pathway that went away from the kitchen and toward my fellow night owl. By taking that path I forever changed the course of my own life. That simple choice set into motion a chain of events that helped to determine where I would go, whom I would marry and the writing of this book. As I walked toward this figure, I notice several things. He seemed slightly shorter than me, and he wore a long monk's robe with a cowl over his head, I never saw a face. As I approached from behind, I could only see the back of his head, the candle in his right hand and the robe. My thought was that this was a member of the monastery, although Franciscan monks of today are more apt to wear blue jeans and sweat shirts. I was about seven feet from the figure when he simply vanished into thin air. There weren't any special effects to account for this; he just wasn't there anymore.

For a long moment I just stood there with wide-eyed wonderment. It then dawned on me that this must be one of those ghosts that people talk about. Then and only then is when I became frightened. I lost my appetite and went to my room and I could not stop shaking. The image of this figure kept haunting me in my mind over and over again. After this encounter, I could not sleep, I left the light on all night. When I spoke with Brother Tim, a monk at the mission, he told me that several other spectres have been seen over the years.

They include a headless woman who rides a horse on moonlit nights and vanishes before she reaches the church. The legend starts during the Gold Rush Era. At that time a Yankee miner fell in love with an Indian maiden who lived in Jolon, not far from the old mission. He married her and built her a comfortable adobe house and bought her a beautiful white horse. He tried to become a farmer but he found the call of the mines too great. At last he told his wife he had to return to try his luck in the gold fields. He left for five long months of hard work. At last he struck it rich. His saddlebags full of gold he rode south to rejoin his young wife. He didn't stop to rest but pressed on in the light of the full moon to his home. When he walked into the bedroom he found his wife with an Indian man. He seized the kitchen ax used to cut fire wood and killed both his wife and the man. Then, insane with blood lust, he cut off his wife's head and took it with him. Seeing the beautiful horse he had given to her he took the bloody ax and killed the poor animal. He rode off into the night still clutching the awful head. From that time on the headless woman, mounted on her white horse has been seen on the road going towards the old Mission San Antonio where some believe she is buried. There is also a ball of light near a grave in the courtyard where strange events had taken place.

During our stay at the mission (June 18th to July 7th) one other member of the team, Troy _______, reported seeing a light. It came into his room (next to mine) and it pinned him to his bed for a few moments. He was very frightened, but he insisted it was only a pinched nerve. I will admit that I heard the bed creak and groan on those nights when no one was in that room. Brother Tim told the ghost stories on June 22. From then on I felt at ease in the old mission. I did not feel "watched" or "spooked." It was this moving experience that motivated me to study the phenomena of ghosts and haunted sites. Even today, the image of the form holding the candle is fresh in my mind. Since that day I have traveled far, toured many haunted places, attended countless seances, interviewed hundreds of witnesses and, yes, even encountered a number ghosts, but the first shall always be the most profound.

About the Author

Richard Leonard Senate was born April 23, 1948, in Los Angeles, CA. The Senate family moved to Ventura County in 1951. Except for three years while attending college, Mr. Senate has been a lifelong resident of the County of Ventura.

Richard Senate has earned a degree in History and has studied Anthropology and Archaeology. The institutes that he had attended are Ventura Community College, Long Beach State University and the University of California Santa Barbara.

In 1978, while taking part in an archaeological excavation at the Mission San Antonio de Padua, near King City, CA., Richard encountered a ghost. This spectre appeared as a monk who was garbed in a robe and cowl. This unexpected encounter began his career in psychic research.

It was in 1983 that Richard met his wife, Debbie Lynn Christenson, and two years later they were wed. She is a gifted psychic and assists in ghost hunts that are conducted throughout California, at no charge.

Both Richard and Debbie are columnists for the County and Coast Reporter Newspaper, a free publication available at many commercial establishments in the City of Ventura. Richard Senate teaches a class that explores the paranormal and is offered by Community Services at Ventura Community College.

About the Illustrator

Sandra Doro Lara was born in Bethesda, Maryland on March 5, 1972.

Since then she has traveled all over the world, living in Washington D.C., Key West ,Bermuda, Virginia, Iceland and Norway before coming to California.

She is a graduate of Channel Islands High School, Ventura Community College and is attending the Art Center College of Design in Pasadena.

She began her career as an artist doing illustrations for her high school newspaper and plans a career as an illustrator.

She resides in Oxnard, California, with her two cats, "Tiger" and "White Star".

What to do if you see a ghost...

1. Don't panic, sit back and enjoy the phenomenon, try to notice all the details that you can.
2. After the event, sit down and write down exactly what you saw.
3. Try to draw a picture of the ghost. What was it wearing? The style of clothing can provide a clue to the era the ghost is from.
4. Draw a map of where the ghost was seen and where you were during the sighting. What time was it?
5. Question others who live in the house or work in the business and see if they have seen anything like the ghost you have witnessed.
6. How did you feel when you saw the ghost?
7. Try to investigate the ghost and discover who it is and why they are haunting the site.

INDEX